Building and Using
Our Sun-Heated Greenhouse

"Who loves a garden, loves a greenhouse too."

William Cowper, *The Task*, 1785

Building and Using
Our Sun-Heated Greenhouse

Grow Vegetables All Year-Round

by

Helen and Scott Nearing

Photographs by Richard Garrett

GARDEN WAY PUBLISHING
CHARLOTTE, VERMONT 05445

Photographs by Richard Garrett
Design and layout by David Robinson
Cover design by Trezzo/Braren Studio

Printed in the United States by Queen City Printers Inc.
Burlington, Vermont
First printing, October 1977

Library of Congress Cataloging in Publication Data

Nearing, Helen.
  Building and using our sun-heated greenhouse.

  1. Solar greenhouses—Design and construction.
2. Greenhouse gardening. 3 Vegetable gardening.
4. Organic gardening. I. Nearing, Scott, 1883–
joint author. II. Title.
SB415N36   635'.04'44   77-13234
ISBN 0-88266-112-4
ISBN 0-88266-111-6 pbk.

Contents

"I have thought good to present your patience with this little volume of varieties, in which, though the title promise no matter of great worth, yet it may be, if you peruse it, you shall find somewhat that you may like in it."

Nicholas Breton, *The Twelve Moneths*, 1626

"The use and application of this Worke, gentle Reader, is to reduce the hard, Barren and Sterile grounds, such as were never fruitful, or such as have been fruitful and are made barren by ill husbandry, to be generally as fruitful as any ground whatsover."

Gervase Markham, *Farewell to Husbandry*, 1649

"To own a bit of ground, to scratch it with a hoe, to plant seeds, and watch the renewal of life—this is the commonest delight of the race, the most satisfactory thing a man can do."

Charles Dudley Warner, *My Summer in a Garden*, 1870

Introduction

We are not professional gardeners. We are homesteaders growing our own food. We are amateurs and lovers of gardening and have been at it for close to half a century.

We have raised vegetables, fruit, and flowers in New Jersey, Pennsylvania, Delaware, Vermont, and Maine, and have helped in gardens in Florida, California, the Netherlands, France, and India.

We have chosen to live in New England for the past forty-five years and have grown accustomed to the vagaries and difficulties of the climate. We delight in the changing seasons. As Henry Thoreau said in *Walden,* "Every season seems best to us in its turn," although we might even prefer the austere, white, isolated winters to the bland, greener, more accessible times of the year.

Happily Adapted

We have happily adapted to the soil and climate of New England, where a short growing season and fierce winters limit our possibilities and strain our ingenuity to garden all year round.

"But how can you garden in sub-zero temperatures and under snow?" is the usual incredulous query. Well, we managed in Vermont, with temperatures ranging down to 45

1

2

degrees below zero, and we manage now in Maine, where the thermometer sometimes registers down to 25 degrees below.

In the spring, summer, and fall our stone wall–enclosed quarter-acre garden supplies us with enough green stuff to feed half a dozen people. Come winter, with snow deep on the ground, we eat the cellar-stored carrots, beets, potatoes, turnips, onions, rutabagas, and apples; the bottled tomatoes, applesauce, vegetable and fruit juices—all garnered from our own place.

Our supplementary source, for growing garden greens all winter, is our sun-heated greenhouse. This glassed-in, otherwise unheated building enables us to extend the balmy spring-summer, summer-autumn months into the tougher, more challenging fall-winter and winter-spring periods. In our greenhouse we grow green things, without artificial heat, through bleak and chilly Novembers into the below-zero temperatures of December, January, and February through blustery March and into April, when the outside garden opens up again.

Plant the Year-Round

Most of our native neighbors in Vermont and Maine get out their seeds and "plant garden" around Memorial Day (May 30) and stop planting in the hot dog days of July. We plant the year-round: first in the greenhouse, then in the garden, and then back in the greenhouse again. In this way we extend our gardening through the four or five months of a likely frigid winter.

Our initial gardening experiences in Vermont, forty-odd years ago, were conventional. We did as the neighboring natives did, planted what they did and when they did. Then we started to branch out. Through various processes we built up the soil to a high fertility level, after years if not generations of consistent neglect.

We built compost piles of our house wastes, our weeds, leaves, and mowings. Few of our neighbors bothered to do that. We mulched much of our garden. We thinned and transplanted more than the usual custom. We kept our garden practically weed-free by hand-cultivating after every rain (thereby exercising weed birth-control). We refrained from dusting and spraying our garden greens, believing that "insecticides and pesticides are a far greater threat to humanity than the atomic bomb."*

Good and Ample Crops

In this way we raised good and ample crops and came close to reaching agricultural self-sufficiency during the brief eighty-five frost-free days that spanned our short Vermont summer, when we could have light night frosts until late June and occasionally into early July. At the other end of the growing season we had an occasional frost that turned potato vines black as early as August 25. Our weather cycle came close to the Vermont farmer's description of his year as "eleven months of winter and thirty days of damn cold weather."

* Dr. Carl C. Wahl, *Essential Health Knowledge,* 1966.

How could we utilize the cold months by continuing to garden through the deep-freeze when the open ground was so hard-frozen that a pickaxe could do little more than flake the surface?

In our early days in Vermont we did not even toy with the idea of a greenhouse. First, we did not have the money to sink in such a project, and second, electricity (which we thought a greenhouse should surely have) had not yet come into our remote valley.

Build Cold Frames

We did build cold frames, put together with old storm windows. Then we thought we might utilize the high south-facing wall of a stone toolshed and put glass in front of that. So evolved our first walk-in greenhouse and our first stab at extending the summer months into winter for our growing plants.

A "green house" it could be from mid-April until mid-October. But could the name "green" be justly applied to any unheated building during the notorious New England winter? How about the other four or five months from November to early April? Would it be possible to depend on a greenhouse without artificial heat during this period? Spring gardening had been recognized as hazardous but possible. Summer gardening was a surety. Fall gardening could extend into October with certain hardy plants. But winter gardening, in a winter greenhouse, seemed like a contradiction of terms, unless the building was heated by more than the sun.

The greenhouse, a corner of the garden.

There are at least a dozen weeks in a New England gardening season when temperatures hover around or below freezing. The point for us has been to find a means of keeping the maximum number of green plants succulent and edible despite the severity of such a winter. We set ourselves to find out ways in which we could lengthen the period of each year during which we might add to our fresh vegetable season. A homemade, unheated greenhouse provided exactly the needed protection for many plants inside its four walls.

Almost by Accident

We began our winter gardening in an unheated greenhouse almost by accident. A small seedling (or seed) got lost under a bench, and in early January, going by chance into the ice-cold building, we found a flourishing, lush, and sizable lettuce plant growing through a clump of dry leaves. It had survived, unwatered and untended, through several months of outside freezing, in a sheltered but chill corner of a cold glassed-in building. If this could happen, uncared for and unbeknownst, why could not more lettuces, and other plants, survive, under better conditions, still without artificial heat? We were launched on an experimental period of greenhouse building and planting that has provided us with fresh green things through thirty winters of freezing and below-zero weather.

Without question, plant germination and growth is checked by cold weather, and only certain plants can survive. Very low temperatures will kill almost any growing thing eventually. But there is a wide margin, and our experiments pointed up the plants that will not be killed by low temperatures. We have been finding out which plants will survive.

We were timid in the beginning of our early experiments with winter gardening. Getting up around daylight and going into the greenhouse at the point of maximum possible frost damage, we saw plants of lettuce and Chinese cabbage and celery, escarole, collards, chard and radishes limp and wilted as though their life span were near its end. Going back a few hours later, after the sun had an hour or two to melt the frost on the greenhouse roof and windows, we found the semi-wilted plants revived, standing up sturdy and strong.

Timid in the Beginning

After a few such experiences we realized that we had seriously underrated the frost-resistant capacity of semi-hardy plants. If a greenhouse looks like a graveyard early on a zero morning, close the door, wait until the sun has burned off the frost covering, and you may be astonished to observe the comeback.

We have been away for weeks or months on end and come back to what we considered disaster in the greenhouse due to windows having been broken or doors left open. A few hours, a few days, or even weeks later, we have found many of the plants vital and growing.

Survive to Be Edible

In the outside garden, leafy vegetables such as kale, Brussels sprouts, Chinese cabbage and many of the hardy root crops temporarily "freeze" during winter weather in cold climates but survive to be edible in the spring. Allow these vegetables to remain in the ground and thaw out gradually and their flavor is even improved, their sugar content increased, and their availability for the winter and early spring menu will be in no way diminished.

Adequate snow coverage in the open garden will often provide a warm blanket against hard freezing, if there is enough dry snow and if it comes before heavy freezing. On one occasion we had two long rows of spinach across the width of our garden. An early snow buried both rows. We were sure we had lost them and put them out of mind. The winter was long and hard. All through January and February the snow remained without a thaw, disappearing only in early March. As the snow went, spinach leaves began to appear. In a few days, to our utter amazement, the two rows of spinach stood up with practically no losses in the rows. Our spinach was months ahead of seed not yet planted by the neighbors.

Was this a miracle? By no means. An early continuous covering of deep dry snow assures the survival of hardy greens like spinach unharmed even in sub-zero weather. This point was underlined for us on another occasion when an outside bed of Boston lettuce came through a snowy winter with only a few losses.

Provide Enough Protection

If certain plants can survive the rigors of sub-zero weather out in the garden, why can they not do as well, or better, in a protected, though cold, building? Though not a perfect proof against winter hazards, unheated greenhouses do provide enough protection to save many plants that otherwise would be finished off in winter storms.

Vegetables in the open garden must face the rough-and-tumble of winter in the North Temperate Zone. Alternate freezings and thawings, high winds, heavy snow drifts, the conversion of wet snow by a drop of temperature into solid and heavy ice, can kill the sturdiest plants. A well-built greenhouse, even if unheated, will shield plants against all of these changes except the severe decrease of temperature. This protection is sometimes sufficient to make the difference between survival and destruction.

We do not want to raise false hopes or predict miracles. We only know that plants hardened off gradually in the open garden or in an unheated greenhouse will tolerate lower and lower temperatures even if the mercury drops below freezing. Each plant has a capacity to adapt itself to changing conditions. If the change is sudden and drastic, the plant may be destroyed. But if the change is gradual, allowing the plant to adapt itself to the alterations, there is no doubt in our minds concerning the ability of many plants to make the adjustment needed for their survival.

High Degree of Adaptability

If plants are kept heated and then suddenly subjected to sub-freezing temperatures, they undoubtedly suffer frost damage and perish. It is the extent, the frequency, the duration of change that must be considered. In the course of a hardening process the resistance of our plants to frost has been notably increased. In our experiments we have been surprised and delighted by the high degree of adaptability possessed by lettuces, spinach, chard, parsley, leeks, and escarole to adjust to new and severe frost conditions.

"It is said land under glass is fifty times more productive of garden crops than open ground. Glass is certainly the solution of the raw winter greens problem. For with no more than the two-sash hotbed in which we start tomato, pepper, and other seedlings, we can eke out the fall lettuce supply until after Christmas."

Henry Tetlow, *We Farm for a Hobby*, 1938

1

What is a greenhouse and why?

Our greenhouse is not an isolated unit; it is an enclosed section of the garden. In the course of time it has met a wide variety of unusual demands and special needs. Each year it is divided and subdivided to meet the requirements of different seeds, different plants, different seasons.

Someone comes along and says: "I have a large pot of rosemary for which I have no place in the winter. Can I put it here in the corner out of your way?" At the lowest side are some stray comfrey plants; there is a pot of geraniums. Part of the greenhouse is full of seed flats of lettuce ready to be transplanted into the garden. Here are melon plants beginning. So they come and they go. Nothing stays very long.

Open Night and Day

In summer the greenhouse may be open night and day. In winter it is closed tight against the frost. In the fall the greenhouse is packed with plants that started growing outside in the summer heat and which we hope to carry into the winter. In late winter there will be dozens of plants that have survived the extreme cold. In late spring the greenhouse will be filled with plants eager to get out into the early sunshine. All summer it will house a hundred or so tomato and green pepper plants that welcome the warmth a glass cover supplies.

Speaking generally, a greenhouse is a structure or device which prevents or postpones frost damage, thus enabling plants to extend their life cycle and remain green. A greenhouse involves the effort to trap and hold heat, and where possible, to increase it. Small glass domes (cloches) are miniature greenhouses; so are cold frames and hotbeds of various shapes and sizes. Beyond these are larger structures, of glass or plastic, sometimes covering acres of land. All of these devices aim to keep out cold air, especially night air, while they aim to admit sunlight through some type of transparent covering. Most of them involve some type of artificial heating.

Problem of Protection

The problem of protection against light or heavy freezing has plagued Temperate Zone gardeners ever since the ending of the Ice Age made gardening possible. With the coming of autumn, unless plants receive adequate protection against Jack Frost, severe drops in temperatures finish them off. There are, of course, perennials, grasses, shrubs and trees which stay green right through the coldest weather. They are called "evergreens."

Under climatic conditions that ensure only 100 frost-free days and nights, with 265 possible frosty inroads, any Temperate Zone homesteader or gardener who is trying to live on home-grown greens must make serious efforts to lengthen the period during which garden greens may be stored or grown.

Outside, the soil rests, but inside, crops reach upward toward the sun.

Some Humans Hibernate

In dealing with cold weather, bears and other animals solve the problem of food supply throughout the winter months by sleeping through the cold weather—by hibernating. Some humans hibernate in southern regions. Others of us attempt to provide ourselves with fresh green food for the largest possible part of each year, even in a cold climate. We could run away from Jack Frost, or we could adapt to the climate and rely on plants which can survive lower temperatures.

Should we Temperate Zone gardeners take nature as we find it and bow to the dictates of temperature, leaving only a very short period available to grow our food? Should we eat out of the cellar or the freezer or the supermarket all winter? Or should we try, in one way or another, to extend the short growing season?

Friends in California, Florida, and Mexico have suggested that we move to warmer, more equable climes, and have even offered us land on which to build. Year after year we have listened to their arguments. After mature consideration we are casting our lot with the snow birds.

We Intend to Stay

We have just built a new stone house on the rockbound coast of Maine. We intend to stay. We have decided to go on living in New England, accepting its soil, its climate, and making the best of each season as it comes along. We will adapt our plant varieties, types of seed and methods of culture to the existing climate. We will garden through the warm months and let a greenhouse meet the needs for fresh greens in winter. An unheated greenhouse is one of the essential features of our program.

People with ample means can have greenhouses built, heated, ventilated automatically, and watered with fine sprays. Generally such folk are interested in producing flowers and rare plants, not ordinary vegetables. Also, and this is of the greatest consequence, often they are spending as much heat-energy on warming their greenhouses as they spend in heating their homes.

We are homesteaders of limited means and are writing for such. Yet we wish to continue a varied green diet during the

In early spring the greenhouse is crowded with greens that have grown through the winter, seedlings nearly ready to be moved into the garden.

Six-foot saplings frame the many compost piles that will offer their fertility to the garden crops.

lean winter months. We homesteaders lack the means to provide artificial greenhouse heat, or we do not have electricity, or we do not choose to use energy that way. We must be content with what heat the sun sends. But in New England we suffer from sunlessness, with clouds, rain, and snow as well as low temperatures prevalent for a large part of the year. Here on the coast we have the added problem of much fog and early morning mist.

Almost all of our gardening experience has been in the North Temperate Zone, taking advantage of summer sunshine when we can get it, and taking cover as cold blasts from the north and east strip the foliage from trees and crumple down green crops in the garden. One of our chief aims in gardening is to find those plants that can remain succulent and edible throughout the coldest weather.

Most cultivated garden plants freeze easily. A garden of beans, corn, tomatoes, and squash can be wiped out by three or four 28° night temperatures. Other garden plants such as Chinese cabbage, some lettuces and celery often can stand up against temperatures as low as 20°. For years we have been able to carry over kale, Brussels sprouts, leeks, parsley, and even spinach in the open garden if a blanket of snow comes before the deep freeze.

Freeze Easily

The winter of 1976–77 was one of the longest continued cold spells, with no alleviating thaws, that we remember. The cold started in November and carried on through to March. We had to leave our farm early in December for a lecture trip and did not return till late January. We found two broken windows in our greenhouse and one of the garden gates wide open and frozen in solid ice. Nevertheless, our sun-heated greenhouse, minus two broken-out windows, and heated only by a few days of pallid sun, was able to supply us with:

1. About 100 elephant leeks, still edible and delicious in mid-February,
2. Several dozen celeriac roots,
3. Two dozen roots of viable green parsley,

4. A score of Pascal celery plants. The outer leaf stems were frozen, but the growing centers were lively and green,

5. A dozen small escarole plants that were lightly covered with dry autumn leaves,

6. Several dozen half-grown lettuce plants: Simpson, Oak Leaf, and Buttercrunch,

7. Three red chard plants.

This is hardly noteworthy in comparison with the glorious green that has carried over for us some winters, but it shows what might be done in a winter greenhouse by gardeners who stayed at home and took care of their winter gardening. We do not recommend leaving a greenhouse without care. We believe that if it is given daily attention the plants which it shelters will be in better condition than if left in total neglect. What we are propounding is the apparent capacity of certain untended plants to survive in continuous sub-zero weather.

The simple, cheap, unheated type of greenhouse that we have evolved adequately protects certain selected greens all winter. With moderate heat in the garden in summer and glass protection through the coldest of the winter months, we have lengthened the season so that we can feed ourselves year-round on growing green things. It is on the basis of almost half a century of experience with growing lettuce and other plants in a cold climate that we base our argument concerning the possibility of year-round gardening in New England and especially the possibility in a glass-walled unheated greenhouse.

" 'Tis merry, merry in the spring,
     And merry in the summer time,
   And merry when the great winds sing
     Through autumn's woodlands brown—
   And in the winter, wild and cold,
     'Tis merry, merry too."

William Howitt, *Good in All Seasons*, 1850

2

Extending the growing season

There are many weeks in a New England gardening season when temperatures hover around freezing. A spring fog or an autumn haze holds the temperature at or near freezing. We guess that during the 120 days from April 1 to June 10 and from August 25 to October 15, our garden may have around five killing frosts and another dozen mornings with white frosts on garden paths. Any one of the killing frosts will eliminate or cripple sensitive seedlings. All of the near-frost nights will retard germination and growth.

A can, bottle, box, or basket, or even some newspaper or a light mulch over each exposed plant will tend to reduce the frost damage, but a greenhouse provides exactly the needed protection for everything inside its four walls. If we have perhaps 105 frost-free days and another 120 days during which a bit of glass will ward off frost damage, an unheated greenhouse in our climate belt will provide adequate frost protection for at least 32 weeks of the 52-week year.

While we were still gardening under the old limits, from Decoration Day in May to Labor Day, our possibilities of producing a year-round food supply were severely restricted. A

Severely Restricted

23

greenhouse doubles the frost-free period, so that we can have frost-free gardening elbowroom for at least two-thirds of every year.

Let us be specific. Despite some twelve weeks per year during which the outside garden will be frozen, the greenhouse can continue to provide many items of home-grown good things. We begin with foliage—green leaves.

1. A bed of wheat, rye, millet, rape, and parsley, if covered with two inches of autumn leaves and a few evergreen branches, will provide succulent green leafage right through the deep freeze period. During the coldest period of the winter we can use the tender young shoots in soup or salad.

2. Roots left in the outside ground may live through periods of extreme cold and continue to be edible. They will survive even better in the greenhouse and be more readily available. The gardener can take carrots or some other root crop before the soil outside is frozen, stake out a small area in the greenhouse floor (say, two by three feet), clip off the growing tops in the ordinary way for storage, use a crowbar to make a hole slightly larger than the root being moved, and drop the root into the hole, root down. The root should fill the hole snugly, with the top about two inches below the soil surface.

Repeat this operation with the roots set apart about two inches by two inches. When the area is filled with replanted roots, scatter a basket of autumn leaves over it, making a

*There's little space for **walking in the tight rows** of the greenhouse.*

two-inch mulch over the entire bed. A couple of small branches will hold the leaves in place. The carrots or celeriac may be dug out at any time during the cold weather. They will never freeze and seldom rot. The same procedure may be followed with almost a dozen winter roots, such as turnips, beets, parsnips, oyster plant (salsify), and winter radishes.

3.   Mature or nearly mature plants may be removed from the open garden and re-set or "heeled" into the greenhouse when hard freezing begins. In our Chapter 10, on our winter greenhouse, this matter will be treated in detail. We mention it here because it is one of the important ways in which a greenhouse lengthens the period of each year during which homesteaders and home gardeners can add to the length of their fresh vegetable season.

4. Kitchen garden herbs in the greenhouse will survive all but the coldest of winters if partially covered with autumn leaves. We have wintered rosemary, thyme, hyssop, and other herbs through the cold season, year after year.

5. Weeks before vegetable or flower seeds can be planted in the open spring garden they can be planted in the green-house, either in the greenhouse ground or in flats. These early plantings include mustard, garden cress, leaf lettuce, early cabbage, and radishes. We can use the thinnings of these tiny emerging plants for salad and we can transplant some at least into the outside garden in late spring. But more of this in Chapter 7 on a spring greenhouse.

To show you more specifically how a greenhouse extends the growing season, we might tell you what the greenhouse looks like just before spring breaks. Let us begin with an inventory of greenhouse produce as the winter of 1975 moved into the spring of 1976.

Planting of Leeks

The largest single element in the greenhouse was a planting of leeks that was raised from seed in the 1975 spring green-house, transplanted into the open garden in April-May of 1975, and re-transplanted as large leeks into the greenhouse in the late autumn of 1975. About a hundred of these mature plants were taken up and "heeled in" as we will describe in Chapter 10. They stayed in the greenhouse through the winter, where they were subject to the usual freezing and thawing of winter weather. All through the winter and spring we were able to dig out the leeks and make good soups as we wanted them.

During the 1975–76 winter the temperature frequently dropped below zero. One morning, if we remember correctly, the thermometer registered 18 degrees below zero. At that level of the mercury one would think the leeks would be frozen stiff. They were. But not a single leek died or rotted. Every leek survived and was green, growing, and edible.

We continue our inventory of the 1976 spring greenhouse by turning to the parsley bed. Parsley seeds germinate slowly and reluctantly. It would have taken several weeks to plant a new parsley seed-flat and have transplants ready for the fall greenhouse. We had no recourse in the autumn of 1975 except to take mature plants from the parsley bed in the open garden. So we looked over our rows for some half-grown plants.

Tricky to Transplant

Parsley plants are notoriously tricky to transplant on account of the scarcity of hair-like feeding roots on the long main root system. Warned by experience, we took the utmost care to select the healthiest parsley plants, lifted them carefully, keeping the largest possible volume of earth hanging to the roots, and moved them, plant by plant, each in its shovel of garden soil, from garden to greenhouse.

In the greenhouse we made a bed of twenty parsley plants, set in a rectangle with six or seven inches between plants. We gently pruned off with our fingers the larger leaves, cutting the foliage to about half of its previous size. After watering the plants carefully we left them to their great adventure of facing life in an unheated greenhouse through a Maine winter which would surely have frozen them in the open.

All twenty of the parsley transplants survived the winter, providing us meanwhile with sprigs for soup and salad. With the coming of spring the plants spurted into a new lease on life and put out new leaf buds and side stalks that would grow into the second and final year of parsley plant life.

In the 1975–76 winter greenhouse we had a bed of celery root or celeriac. Celery is generally not winter-hardy; celeriac is more so, but we had had little success the preceding year in storing celeriac in our root cellar along with the potatoes, carrots, beets, and rutabagas. We therefore decided to experiment a bit, taking up the celeriac roots in the fall, stripping off most of their leaves, and heeling them into the winter greenhouse. The transplantation was successful and we were still eating celeriac roots when spring came in 1976.

A Bed of Celeriac

We stress our experience with leeks and parsley, carrots and celeriac, because it illustrates the principle we are advancing. It is quite possible to carry a sun-heated greenhouse full of growing vegetation right through weeks of deep freeze, and many of them on into the open weather that follows the spring thaw.

Our year-round greenhouse continually contains a wide variety of plants; some more hardy, some less. In it at each season—spring, summer, autumn, winter—there are plants in various stages of development. Seeds, tiny seedlings, or mature plants occupy every square foot of the greenhouse. Some seeds, recently sowed, are not yet germinated. Some will make the salad for the day's evening meal. Some, like tomatoes or peppers, remain in the greenhouse for months. All these plants, in various stages, will be transplanted, consumed, and replaced in their turn. Before the greenhouse soil gets its next crop of plants or seeds, it will be reworked, refertilized, and either re-

Variety of Plants

seeded or occupied by seedlings raised in another section of the greenhouse, and re-set in the recently vacated soil.

Each month and season will find some variety of plant life playing its allocated role in providing the edibles that make up our daily diet. The sequences are carefully planned to produce the maximum in food value from each square foot of greenhouse soil, and all tend to extend the growing season.

"I had rather not to build a mansion or a house, than to build one without a good prospect in it, to it, and from it. For and the eye be not satisfied, the mind can not be contented."

Andrew Boorde, *The Dyetary of Helth,* 1542

3

Locating the greenhouse

Great care should be taken in locating the greenhouse. It is an integral part of the garden and should be treated as such. Homesteaders' greenhouses, being a part of the productive chain, are enclosed sections of the gardening area. They should be handy to the garden so that the gardener can pass from garden to greenhouse and from greenhouse to garden with the least loss of time and effort. If the garden is enclosed by a wall or fence, the greenhouse should be included within that enclosure.

In earlier days, heated greenhouses or conservatories for flowers and exotic plants were to be found attached to the dwellings in all well-appointed country estates. Later the greenhouse became one aspect of truck farming. Today, in the North Temperate Zone, the greenhouse is becoming one link in the chain that supplies fresh green food for homesteaders, an extension of their living and farming quarters.

Face to the South

The greenhouse should face to the south. It should be so located that the rays of the early spring sun strike as directly as possible on the greenhouse roof and other glass-covered areas. The more direct the sun's rays, the more will the greenhouse plants benefit from the warmth of early spring sunshine.

33

A successful greenhouse cannot be built where shade trees such as elms, maples, oaks, or evergreens occupy a large proportion of the landscape. There is no substitute for all the sun that plants can get. At every stage of their growth and development they require sunlight.

In locating a greenhouse there may come a time when the owner of a favorite tree has to choose between the tree and a greenhouse, if the tree shades the selected spot. The tree owner and the would-be owner of the greenhouse must decide: greenhouse or tree, tree or greenhouse; one or the other, not both.

The greenhouse should be open to the sun on the south and west.* Similarly, it should be closed against the cold weather which blows in from the north and east. The north side of the greenhouse should be designed to take full advantage of the south side of a wall.

If the north wall of your greenhouse is wooden, the inside can be painted black with a paint that is not injurious to vegetation. It will thereby absorb more heat during the day and radiate more warmth at night.

Barrier Against Cold

It may be possible to use some outbuilding as a barrier against cold winds. Here in Maine we have used the south side of a stone-walled garage. In Vermont we used the south side of a stone tool–storage building.

---

* "For garden best is south southwest," says old Thomas Tusser in *Five Hundreth Pointes of Good Husbandrie, 1557.*

Helen and Scott Nearing work together on a stone wall, filling wooden forms that can be reused again and again.

To take advantage of house-heating, many greenhouse builders have located their greenhouse facilities in a window or door frame on the south side of their homes. The plants, however, get used to the heat and lose their adaptation to the cold. They no longer live in a purely sun-heated greenhouse.

Well Drained

Greenhouse soil should be well drained at all times. Never should there be the possibility of standing water or of soil so wet that it forms cakes or balls when cultivated. Run-off water should drain away from the greenhouse on at least two sides.

Water searches constantly for a lower level. Any portion of a piece of land that has clay or basic rock foundation would attract moisture twenty-four hours in every day. If a greenhouse confronted no other obstacles beyond drainage we would hesitate a long time before borrowing trouble by placing it where its feet would be constantly wet.

In early spring, when moisture is generally abundant and sun heat is at a minimum, there is always a possibility that mould and rot will get started in enclosed damp earth. At this point in the growing season the gardener should be able to work the surface of the recently frozen earth, to air it and to have it warmed by the still weak sun of early spring. Under these conditions the drier the garden surface the warmer the earth and the greater the chance for early seed germination and plant growth.

Pointing the walls means filling the spaces between stones with rich mortar.

We are laying special emphasis on this point because we are convinced that many greenhouse difficulties and losses are due to an excess of moisture rather than to moisture shortage. This is notably true of sunless and cold periods.

Pit Greenhouse

Advocates of a pit greenhouse favor a greenhouse floor below the level of the garden. They base their advocacy on the assumption that if the greenhouse is built below the level of the surrounding soil it will be freed from sharp temperature variations and will benefit from the underground heat of the earth.

Certainly the earth temperature below frost penetration is relatively constant, as between the seasonal changes of above ground, from summer to winter and back again. To secure that advantage the greenhouse builder must dig a pit from many inches to several feet deep depending on the local depth of frost level. Where we live in Maine this would be three to four feet. Such an operation has some drawbacks.

First, it is expensive in time and labor to dig out a cellar hole of such dimensions and to find an effective way of placing and distributing so much subsoil.

Second, a hole of these dimensions would extend well into the subsoil. Our topsoil here being less than a foot in depth, if we went down into the subsoil two feet, the entire greenhouse would have a floor of subsoil. Since we cannot grow crops in yellow clay, it would be necessary to replace a foot of yellow clay by at least a foot of fertile garden soil—another time-consuming operation.

Third, unless the greenhouse is built on a steep slope, rain-water and melting snow would run or seep into the greenhouse, creating a flooding hazard. Even in the absence of surplus water, such an excavation would tend to catch and hold moisture with the consequent tendency to create a swamp. At the very least it would be necessary to maintain a pumping system to counter the water hazard.

Every homesteader who builds a greenhouse confronts a different situation. We have tried to list some of the important factors in greenhouse location. Greenhouse builders can survey their peculiar situations in the light of our suggestions.

"A man must consider the expense before he do begin to build; for there goeth to building many a nail, many pins, many laths and many tiles or slates or straws beside other great charges, as timber, boards, lime, sand, stones or brick, beside the workmanship and the implements."

Andrew Boorde, *The Dyetary of Helth*, 1542

4

Building the greenhouse

Greenhouses are not hard to build. They can be easily "home-made" by amateur carpenters and masons. They are simple of construction, usually fairly small buildings, and do not cost much money or time.

We have seen greenhouses of various designs from rectangular to square to circular. For an ordinary homesteading family we suggest a rectangular building with a shed roof. Most farm houses and outbuildings in New England have been and still are rectangular. It will be easier to follow that pattern unless there is some good reason for making a change.

Easiest Way

If you have a building with a blank wall along its south side, the cheapest and easiest way to add a greenhouse is to use the blank wall as the back side of the greenhouse which thereby becomes a "lean-to," with a single pitch roof sloping away from the windbreak.

On its higher side, the greenhouse should be at least eight feet high. If you are building in cold country, be sure that the pitch of the roof is enough to permit easy snow removal. With a small building, the weight of the snow is not a serious problem, but the presence of any snow on the greenhouse roof prevents sun rays from reaching the greenhouse floor.

43

Snow

Snow anywhere about the greenhouse will hold down the temperature. As soon as possible after snow falls, remove it from the greenhouse roof to let in sunlight and sun heat. A small, light, wooden snow-pusher with a long handle can be homemade and will dispose of the snow and let in light and hopefully sunshine.

Snow that is light and fluffy can be pushed off the greenhouse roof at once. If the snow is damp and the air temperature is below freezing, the snow may be frozen onto the glass roof. Only occasionally is this a problem. Ordinarily, in daylight, temperatures inside the greenhouse are higher than outside. If that is the case, snow frozen onto the glass roof is quite temporary. Snow is a warm blanket holding the heat rays inside the greenhouse. As the greenhouse warms up, the snow on the roof softens, melts, and slides easily off the roof. Each use of the pusher detaches some of the snow cover. The pitch of the glass roof takes care of the separate masses which slide quite easily, propelled by gravity.

*These pictures show how panes of glass form the greenhouse roof.
The slope allows snow to be pushed off easily.*

In our experience, if the roof is kept free of snow and ice in
winter, the daytime temperature in a sun-heated greenhouse in
moderately clear weather will be about 20° higher than the
temperature outside the greenhouse. In cloudy, foggy weather
the temperatures inside and outside tend to equalize. On a
bright cold day the temperature inside may be 35° to 40°
higher than outside.

Don't build the greenhouse too big and don't build it too
small. The size should depend on the size of the family and the
general need. Like every additional unit of the homestead, the
greenhouse calls for its share of upkeep, and the smaller it is

the less attention and cost it demands. Glass is breakable; plastic wears out quickly. Build it as large as necessary, but remember that, other things being equal, the smaller the less costly in labor, materials, and upkeep.

Snug Corner

When we planned our Maine greenhouse we made it twenty feet by ten and later lengthened it by twenty more feet. Forty by ten is ample for the average family homestead. Ten by twenty is on the small side. We put the greenhouse on the north side of our garden against the blank wall of our stone garage. With a five-foot garden wall already to the east, our greenhouse is in a snug corner, protected by walls from the north and east winds and with glass on the south and west.

Our finished greenhouse wall was twelve inches in thickness. On each side of the wall we allowed two inches as a footing for our forms, so we made our foundation trench sixteen inches wide. The trench was about forty inches deep, which is sufficient in our area to avoid frost heaves.

Mark the outside limits of the prospective building by driving stakes at the four corners. The stakes should be driven in solidly. If the earth is hard, a metal bar can be used to make holes into which the corner stakes can be driven until they are firm and not easily moved.

If the building is to be ten by twenty feet outside, and if you are allowing for a sixteen-inch trench, your stakes must be 10'4" and 20'4" apart. There is an old saying among builders: "Measure thrice and cut once." It is widely applicable. It

means to check each measurement a sufficient number of times so that there will be no mistakes.

Right Angle

When your distances are correctly measured, see that your angles are equally correct. The sides and ends of the building should not only be the same length but each of the four corners should be a 90° or right angle.

Pick out a straight 2″ x 4″ x 12′ or 2″ x 6″ x 12′. Put this timber along one end of the projected building, peg it firmly into place, using at least three stakes so that there will be little chance of the timber moving sideways. Use a grubbing axe and cut through the sod along the line of the timber from one corner stake to the next. Be careful not to damage the sod, if

such there be. Preserved intact, it can be used to edge the top of the trench, obviating the use of forms at ground level.

The 2″ x 6″ straightedge is then shifted sixteen inches to the other side of the proposed trench, staked in place, and the sod is again cut carefully with the grubbing axe. You are now in a position to remove the sod, using a mattock to loosen it and a spade or flat shovel to lift and roll it into rolls that are light enough to handle easily. The sods may be cut into convenient sizes and any surplus used on a sod pile. The topsoil should also be removed and wheeled to the garden or compost pile.

Remove the Sod

You now have the beginnings of the foundation trench. While digging through the subsoil be careful in removing any rocks encountered in the trench. Some may extend across your shovel line. Expert earth workers are a real treasure at this stage in construction. An experienced worker with earth will have the sides of the foundation trench firm and vertical enough to serve as the form within which the foundation will be built. Your trench walls will provide the forms that will contain the stone and concrete foundation that will support your building.

If the work is being done professionally, a backhoe will be brought in to dig the trenches and they will be left wide and ragged. Wooden forms will have to be built, and a transit-mix truck loaded with concrete will pour the four sides of the proposed foundation in one operation.

Proceed More
Slowly

We self-sufficient homesteaders, with our limited means, will proceed more slowly, do one foundation wall at a time, and end up after several days with a stone and concrete foundation that can carry the new building. We try to dig each trench and fill it on the same day. An open trench is an invitation to erosion. The sooner it is filled the better, both on account of crumbling walls and of children or animals playing or moving about.

As soon as the foundation ditch is dug to the required below-frost-level, we spread four inches of stones about the size of baseballs across the bottom. On top of these stones we pour a soft mixture of concrete: six parts gravel, three parts sand and one part cement. This is mixed in a wheelbarrow with a shovel.

If the homesteader has a concrete mixer, the job can be done faster but our construction motto is "Wisely and slow, they stumble who go fast." We have used mixers, both hand-operated and engine-powered. We prefer mixing with a short-handled shovel in a metal wheelbarrow for most small jobs. We have used only a wheelbarrow and shovel to lay 400 feet of stone wall around our garden, and with only wheelbarrow and shovel we have built our whole new stone house. A concrete mixer requires scraping and washing up after every job. It has to be housed and cared for. We think it is not worth the trouble. If the homesteader enjoys doing first-class work and is willing to spend the time, he will go a bit slower but will have the satisfaction of a good job well done.

Ready for
More Rocks

With the scattered stone floor of the trench covered with the soft mixture, we are ready for more rocks. We bring in boulders of twelve to fourteen inches in diameter, the larger the better so long as they fit into the form. We drop the boulders carefully into place, setting them two or three inches apart, so that they are separated from each other and from the sides of the ditch, but tied together by soft concrete. Throughout this operation we are careful not to knock dirt from the trench wall into the fresh mixture.

We now pour enough sticky concrete to fill the trench halfway to the top of the boulders. We tamp the concrete thoroughly as it is shoveled or dumped into the trench. If our tamping shows any pockets of soft concrete, these pockets are filled with chunky stones, as large as called for but small enough so that no two stones touch. Again we tamp thoroughly until all air pockets are eliminated and add more concrete.

We are now ready to put in our second layer of boulders, always being careful to leave at least two inches of concrete between all stones. Again we tamp, filling in this way until we reach ground level.

Unless we have reached the top of the wall, the rougher the top surface at the end of the working day the better. If more concrete wall will be added on the next work day, the rougher the surface the tighter will the new concrete cling to the old.

We make every effort to construct a solid, dirt-free concrete foundation that will carry the twelve-inch stone and concrete walls of the greenhouse. The object is to secure maximum solidity and stability at a minimum cost. With us, stone,

Movable wooden forms in place.

gravel, and sand all come from our own place, their only cost being the labor needed to fetch and handle them. These "free" materials should play the largest possible role in the foundation construction.

Movable Wooden Forms

Our north and east walls were built with movable wooden forms eighteen inches wide and of varying lengths. We originated the forms and they have become standard with us. They consist of three pine boards each six inches wide. The six-inch boards are held together by 2″ x 3″ spruce studs, spaced twenty-four inches apart, center to center. The end studs on each form have half-inch holes at top and bottom, all made with the same pattern and therefore interchangeable.

Any two form ends may be bolted to the next form (up and down or sideways) by ⅜″ bolts equipped with washers and wing nuts.

The forms, when set in place on the foundation wall, must be exact as to length, level, and plumb. Where necessary they are braced from the outside, forming a box to contain the concrete. The forms are held apart by twelve-inch spacers and held together, top and bottom, by twisted malleable wires, preferably around the studs. Concrete is heavy and the pressure of the soft material is considerable.

Level as Possible

Our procedure is to shovel into the form about two inches of sticky concrete, completely covering the foundation wall. Against the forms we place stones, the larger the better, a flat face to the form, and tucked into the soft concrete. We try to keep the wall, as we lay it, as level as possible, adding one face-stone above the other and supporting them with more concrete. We tamp regularly as we go. As the form fills up we keep the topmost stones below the top of the form, leaving a rough surface to grip the next layer of concrete that will be added with the new form.

When a piece of wall has stood in the forms for forty-eight hours, the concrete is set. Wires are cut, bolts are removed. If concrete is sticking to the forms it is scraped off with a flat shovel and the forms are set at the next level.

After removal of the forms, the sooner the wall is pointed the better. Pointing consists of working with a small trowel and a rich mixture of mortar (three parts fine sifted sand to one part of cement) between the stones showing on the outside of the wall.

Pointing

When the walls approach the planned height, $\frac{1}{2}''$ x $10''$ anchor bolts should be embedded in the concrete, at a level so that $3\frac{1}{2}''$ of each will protrude above the finished wall. They should be spaced six feet apart, starting at one foot from each corner. These will hold the sill. The stone and concrete mixture should be continued up to within an inch or more of the top of the finished wall, and the remainder filled with a rich pointing mixture.

This ends the stone and concrete work. When this finishing layer of concrete has set, and the forms have been removed, a $2''$ x $6''$ sill plate timber is laid on top of the wall and bolted in place, using the anchor bolts.

The framing for the windows is placed on this, and cut to fit the storm windows available to us. The windows are hung so that they open out from the top, and close against a stop on all four sides that provides a reasonably airtight fit.

This window framing is capped with another $2''$ x $6''$ timber, which forms a top plate. The roof rafters ($2''$ x $4''$) are fastened to this plate and extend to another $2''$ x $6''$ timber bolted to the top of the wall at the rear of the greenhouse. This second timber serves as a ridgepole.

The size of glass used decides how far apart the rafters will

be. The glass used on our job was double-strength 16″ x 24″ window glass. If you follow our pattern, placing the runs of glass directly on the rafters, it will be wise to have the rafters of some light and durable wood such as cedar. It will also be wise to have a planer cut the channels in which the glass is to lie.

We began laying the glass at the low side of the roof. A sheet of glass is laid between rafters and fastened into place with small finishing nails or special grommets. The second sheet laps over the first by at least one inch, and so on until the peak of the roof is reached. Putty or prepared glazing compound is then worked along each rafter and piece of glass.

Stone and Concrete

We have written this chapter as though it were necessary to build a greenhouse with stone and concrete. We are under no such illusion. Building with stone happens to be a hobby with us. Most greenhouses are built with wood, and modern commercial ones are increasingly made with a metal frame with glass or some type of glass substitute. We find it fascinating and not difficult to build with stone, though it is admittedly slow work.

This construction gave us a greenhouse space ten feet wide, about eight feet high at the north side and about six and a half feet high on the south. With a forty-foot span from west to east, our greenhouse encloses about 2,800 cubic feet. This is the body of air on which the plants in the greenhouse depend for their livelihood. As this air is warmed through the day, it provides the heat needed for plant growth. After sunset, in cooperation with the stone walls of the greenhouse, which reflect heat, the plants keep warm far into the night.

Stood Up Well

A part of our greenhouse is now almost twenty-five years old. We have lost an occasional sheet of glass, the glazing compound has been replaced several times, but the greenhouse has stood up well.

All Costs Were Minimal

We have been asked how much our greenhouse cost us. We have not kept records on this through the years. We know that all costs were minimal, having done the bulk of the work with our own hands, and with materials from the place. Since we never start a construction job unless we have materials, free time, and money enough in hand to cover necessary outlays, we do not ask how much these projects cost but what they have brought us in experience gained. Every aspect of such a job yields its dividends as it comes along. And as Robert Louis Stevenson noted: "The true success is to labor."

We enjoy each operation in this or any other farm work and tackle it as a series of lessons, whether it is in gardening or in road-making or in forestry. If we went to a school to get our experience we would expect to pay tuition. On this greenhouse job we have learned a great deal, and there was no charge for tuition. At a country club or a gymnasium, in search of exercise, we would have paid dues and got dressed up as the price for fresh air and body movement. On the greenhouse project we had sunshine, fresh air, and invigorating exercise for free. They were dividends that came with the job.

A number of friends lent a hand in building the greenhouse and were recompensed in what ways they wanted, mostly in meals of our home-grown food. If we tried to itemize charges and benefits on paper we would have to note that in the course of doing these cooperative jobs erstwhile strangers have become good friends. Friendship cannot be valued in money nor can it be priced.

The accounts we kept for the greenhouse through the years show benefits of added knowledge, skills, friendly sharing of experience, and the preservation of good health. These results put us high up in the scale of well-being. They are part and parcel of living a good life.

"One hears a lot about the rules of good husbandry; there is only one—leave the land far better than you found it."

George Henderson, *The Farming Ladder*, 1944

5

Soil in the greenhouse

Soil is of supreme importance in all gardening operations. It is the portion of the earth's crust which comes into direct contact with plant life. It is the source of the plant's food and housing. Plant roots, seeking nourishment, usually confine themselves to the few top inches in which the bulk of plant sustenance is to be found.

Topsoil is a mixture of decomposing rock particles and decaying organic substances that supply the necessary nutriments for growing plants. Rock particles and other inert matter not yet mixed with humus or decaying organic matter lie below the topsoil and are called subsoil. This subsoil includes earth particles not sufficiently broken down to be available for plant food. The anchor roots of the plant kingdom penetrate the subsoil deeply as they search for a hold sufficiently strong to enable the plant to stand up against wind, water, and other potentially disturbing factors. It is the topsoil in which they feed.

Yellow Clay Base

Unfortunately for us, the piece of earth on which we put our garden has a yellow clay base, far from a good source of plant food. At the time we were deciding on the location for our garden we had two alternatives: a piece of ground grow-

61

ing poor grass on a sandbank that was six feet or more in depth, and a field of exceedingly healthy weeds, but deep in yellow clay.

Both moisture and fertility would leach down through the sandbank, leaving the topsoil waterless in a dry season and with insufficient fertility. We decided in favor of the yellow clay base because the crop of weeds was so fine and because we thought we could lighten the soil with compost and humus, which we did.

In the long run, soil can be extensively modified and improved, but often at a high cost in labor and materials. Our garden soil in Maine gave us particular problems. And as our greenhouse soil is an extension of the garden (that part of the garden which lies between the greenhouse walls), and at the same level as the garden, it suffers the same disadvantages.

Forest Soil

We did three things to offset the clay in our garden and greenhouse site. The first was to apply a great quantity of alkaline compost. This went a long way to soften the soil and make it more friable. The second input was sand. The third addition was autumn leaves and forest soil. Of the three we think that the leaves and wood dirt have been the most useful.

Whenever we work with forestland we collect any forest floor soil that comes our way. The humus is the brownish or blackened soil which is the upper layer of any long-established forest. It is made up of the native rock particles in which vegetation is growing, plus decomposing leaves, twigs,

A compost pile, ready for the garden.

branches and trunks of trees and the droppings and dead bodies of animals and birds. Occasional dust storms also add to the forest floor.

Each autumn we gather and store dry leaves. Not long ago leaves were generally burned or dumped. Increasingly they are being picked up and treasured by soil initiates as a highly prized element for soil builders.

Leaf Storage Spot

We have a leaf storage spot in an inner corner of a thirteen-inch, seven-foot-high stone wall. Around this inner corner we have set a line of stakes five or six feet from the wall and four or five feet apart. On this stake line we have placed two-inch

mesh galvanized chicken-wire, tied to the stakes with binder twine. This leaf bin sounds flimsy and insecure, but it holds the leaves adequately, is easily taken down when we want leaves, and has served our needs for storage year after year.

We incorporate the leaves into the garden or greenhouse soil at every opportunity, for mulch and for nourishment. Half-rotted leaves from the bottom of the storage bin are added to compost piles and spaded into the soil, spring and fall.

We Are in No Hurry

We do not mention animal manure as a soil conditioner because we do not use it. As vegetarians we do not eat the flesh of our brother animals and we try to exploit them as little as possible. By not utilizing their offal, blood-meal, or the other by-products of the slaughter industry, we make a stand against the slavery of domestic creatures. Animal manure might push our plant growth faster, but we are in no hurry; let others have the first tomatoes or peas or corn. Our crops will feed us in good time. Nature is not in a hurry, nor should we be.

In this connection we should also note the absence of prepared chemical fertilizers in our gardening procedures. As organic gardeners and farmers we rely (like the magnificent and massive redwoods) upon disintegrating rocks and decomposing organic materials for increasing the fertility of our soil. We do use rock powders and earth deposits as a source for increases in the phosphorus, potash, and some trace elements in our soil; none of these is the product of any other treatment beyond grinding or milling.

We prepare our greenhouse soil in the autumn or early winter by spading into it a good inch or two of the semi-rotted leaves and an inch of wood dirt. Above this layer we add two or three inches of well-rotted compost. On top of this we sprinkle some protein meal which we have mixed previously in a wheelbarrow and stored in buckets. It consists of what is available in the market of equal parts of soybean, cottonseed, or seaweed meal, with phosphate rock, granite dust, or dolomite lime. This protein meal is raked into the upper layer of greenhouse soil with a potato hook or other similar tool.

Soil shift and soil renewal are parts of daily greenhouse practice. Of course soil in the greenhouse will be changed from season to season. Each time there is a change of crops the soil should be worked over. Each time fertilizer should be added, aiming to supply the nutriments necessary for the next crop.

Greenhouse Soil

What is an ideal greenhouse soil? The answer to this question will change from one season and one crop to another. In general, however, we would answer that an ideal soil for a homestead greenhouse should be as close as possible to what soil experts call a sandy loam. It should contain a minimum of clay and should be alkaline. It should be friable, so that it runs easily between the fingers, with a relatively high humus content. It should be deep enough to provide ample room for growing root systems to spread and reach down. Chemically, it should contain plenty of nitrogen, phosphorus, and potash,

Scott works hard, likes to.

in properly balanced proportions, together with the widest possible range of trace minerals.

Briefly, the greenhouse soil should advance as much as possible the germination of seed, the formation of abundant root systems, and the ultimate growth, flowering, and fruiting of the plants in question.

We work towards these favorable conditions in our garden and in our greenhouse soil. If not always within our control in the outer garden, within the few square feet of our small homestead greenhouse it can be achieved. A few hours of concentrated time, a small money expenditure, and sufficient fore-sight to have the various necessary ingredients on hand are largely within reach of the average homesteader.

One of the great advantages of greenhouse gardening is that one can deal with the soil in small units. One need not work over all of the greenhouse soil at the same time, because many different operations are going on in the greenhouse. The gardener is able to enrich his greenhouse soil by adding to it fertilizer designed to meet the requirements of the crop or crops which he has on his schedule at a particular point in the calendar year. If the greenhouse gardener proposes to raise a crop such as cucumbers, he can add to a section of greenhouse soil exactly those nourishing elements needed to produce cucumbers.

Production of Young Plants

One major use of a greenhouse is the production of young plants which will be set in the outside garden when weather and other conditions are auspicious. In this operation we use flats, pots, and special greenhouse plots, all of which need special soil preparation.

Into our seed flats and larger outside garden flats we put a prepared soil mixture, consisting of sand, compost, rotted sod, garden soil, and wood dirt, in equal proportions. These are mixed together, sifted, and supplemented by a generous sprinkling of the previously mentioned nitrogen meal. This mixture is put into flats on a base of a half-inch of sphagnum moss, to absorb and retain any excess moisture.

The seed flats are planted, watered moderately, and kept damp (never wet) until the germinating seeds have broken through the ground. The seedlings remain in the seed flats until they have developed a root system that will stand transplanting. At that point they are carefully removed from the seed flats with as much as possible of the root system intact, and planted in the larger garden flats, with a sufficient distance between plants to allow for plant growth and to provide a unit of soil when the plants are moved from the garden flats into the open garden.

To Improve the Soil

Parts of our greenhouse were set aside as a greenhouse area twenty or more years ago. During the intervening years, crop after crop has been taken from the greenhouse and either transplanted or consumed. Following the principle of return on each operation, we add to the net amount of nutriment in the particular unit of soil. At all times we have in mind the basic principle of organic gardening: to put into the soil more fertility than crops or erosion take out. If we want to improve the soil it is necessary to put in more than we remove. As we are taking our plants from the greenhouse and harvesting crops, one after another, at the same time we aim to increase the capacity of the soil to produce further abundant crops of nutritious food.

"Water, light and air, those three physical facts which render existence possible."

John James Ingalls, *Blue Grass*, 1890

6

Light, heat, moisture, air

Fertile, balanced soil is a basic essential for successful greenhouse practice. There are four other factors that play a major role: sunlight, heat, moisture, and air.

Sunlight is the chief requisite for a well-functioning greenhouse. Its importance has been stressed in our chapter on locating the greenhouse. In New England we need all the sun we can get. The purpose of our greenhouse is to trap and retain a maximum amount of sunshine. This holds for every growing day of the year.

Sun Heat

With sunlight comes sun heat. The two provide two of the indispensable elements in gardening. Sunlight is amplified by sun heat. Sun heat may be so intense and prolonged as to raise crops of semi-tropical and even tropical plants in northern greenhouses, but it must then be supplemented for lengthened periods with artificial heat. That is for the rich or for some institution or business. It is outside the income range of most homesteaders, who must content themselves with the share of sunlight and sun heat that reaches their greenhouses from Mother Nature.

71

Moisture is quite a different story. The homesteader is the benign provider who can supply the plants with their necessary quota of moisture. Cut off by walls and roof from natural sources, the plants depend completely on him for their watering.

It goes without saying that the greenhouse must have enough moisture to support plant survival and healthy growth. It is equally true that greenhouse soil, like any other piece of mother earth, can be over-watered. This is particularly true in the case of seed germination and the formation of adequate root systems on young plants. There are cold periods in winter and dry periods in summer and autumn when the moisture levels of a greenhouse are of supreme importance.

Easy to Over-Water

It is easy to over-water a greenhouse. If there is any choice, under-watering is preferable. In a small operation like ours, water may be applied through a hose or with a watering can. We aim always to observe the soil closely and to take steps to keep it damp enough but not too wet. Often we go over exposed greenhouse soil more than once a day, scratching the surface with a tool or stick to form a dust mulch and to see that the soil surface is never damp to the touch. At the same time the soil below the surface should contain sufficient moisture to provide the plant roots with a minimum supply.

Beginners often over-water a greenhouse. Under frost conditions particularly they should follow an opposite policy, based on the formula: the less moisture the better, always providing that the plants receive a moisture quota sufficient to keep them alive and growing. For new greenhouse owners it is necessary to stress the need of maximum dryness in greenhouse gardening.

We learned this lesson early in our experience. Back in the early 1960's we had carried a fine-looking greenhouse garden through December and January into February. Our pride was a bed of half-grown lettuce plants that were beginning to head up. They had stood the test of January's zero nights,

Learned This Lesson Early

thanks to a moderate mulch of autumn leaves. We were count-
ing the days before we could begin eating the robust lettuces.

February brought a three-day thaw. Our prize lettuce
plants, encouraged by the warm sunshine coming through the
greenhouse roof and windows, spread themselves magnificent-
ly. Twice during the thaw we watered them. Our first watering was restrained and careful. The Simpson and Boston
plants benefited so much from this initial watering that the
next day, another warm one, we gave all the lettuce a good
soaking to show our appreciation and to give further encouragement to the plants.

That night the wind shifted to the north and the thermometer dropped to 15 degrees above zero. The next morning our prize lettuce bed was frozen stiff. We did not worry
too much. These plants had been hardened off through several
weeks of zero and near-zero weather. After each bout with
Jack Frost the lettuces had come back, strong and fibrous,
without the loss of a single plant. But throughout this cold

weather stretch they had lived on a meager ration of water, mostly condensation from the roof. They had had maximum dryness and therefore withstood the frost. This time, however, they had been given all the water they could take. They were full of it, and not a single lettuce plant survived the ordeal.

What had happened this time to exterminate our lettuce crop? The answer was simple. The lettuce bed had been living on a level of maximum dryness. Our generous watering had gorged the lettuce leaves with unaccustomed water. The cold night had converted this excessive water supply into ice, bursting the lettuce cells and putting the plants out of business.

We had learned our lesson. A lettuce plant glutted with water cannot survive a hard freeze. From that day forward we have been practicing maximum dryness in every cold period.

Ventilation

If light and warmth are primary essentials of successful greenhouse gardening under possible frost conditions, an equally important conditioning factor is air or ventilation. The temperature of the air, neither too high nor too low, makes it possible for plant life to continue in good health.

Plants breathe. Like so many other life forms, their survival depends upon air—the cleaner and purer the better. Subject to the limitations of temperature, the more fresh air greenhouse plants get, the better. Greenhouse ventilation thus becomes one of the essential features of greenhouse practice.

We open the window sash on the south side of the green-house when the sun is warm, and close the sash by mid-after-noon or when the sun is covered with clouds. The greenhouse sashes on the south side are hinged at the bottom and open at the top. Each sash is provided with a length of woven mason's line, long enough to allow for ventilation and still hold the sash upright. As warm air rises, a small or large opening at the top of the sash provides for air circulation.

Abundant Fresh Air

Since our greenhouse is filled all summer with fruiting tomato plants, eggplants, or some melons, we watch the temperature and close the windows before sundown, thereby holding enough warm air in the greenhouse to offset a possible night chill. If the summers are uniformly hot, we may remove the sashes completely and store them until autumn. Most summers we leave the sashes in position, opening widely enough to pro-vide abundant fresh air.

Each change in weather will have some effect on the humid-ity of greenhouse air. If the weather changes are drastic and frequent, the person responsible for greenhouse well-being must be ready to make correspondingly sudden and drastic changes in the greenhouse situation. Since the weather may change at any hour of the day or night, the conscientious plant-grower must be prepared for what comes.

Even with a feel for the weather or with access to the most up-to-date weather reports, the gardener is likely to be caught

Visitors come to admire and to learn.

napping by the wide variability of New England weather. Mark Twain said, "There's one thing certain about the weather: there'll be plenty of it." Certainly the comment attributed to Emerson holds true: "If you don't like current weather in New England, wait a few minutes."

Sunshine and the moisture content of the earth and the air may be fairly stable, or they may change from hour to hour. Gardeners who are accustomed to stable weather that is reasonably constant day after day, or even week after week, are unprepared for weather that changes while they look at the thermometer, or while they watch the sun ducking in or out of cloud masses, or listen to the rattle of a ten-minute shower on the greenhouse roof.

We do not want to over-emphasize the importance of weather changes, but the careful gardener is forced to take them into consideration every hour of the twenty-four.

In the 1950's and 60's we were spending many winters traveling back and forth across the country from the Atlantic to the Pacific. This kept us away from home for long periods. We left the greenhouse nailed up tight, with no one caring for it. What did we do for ventilation and watering during that time?

One year we had to spend almost five winter months on a trip to Asia, getting home only after spring had opened up. Before leaving the Maine garden we had transplanted 120 young lettuce plants from garden flats into the greenhouse where they were set seven inches apart, with a light mulch of leaves over all. We nailed up the building before we departed and left it alone for the winter. When we returned five months later we found 65 of the 120 lettuce transplants (Oak Leaf, Simpson, and Boston) green and well-headed. We ate fresh lettuce greens for the next month and had plenty to give away to neighbors and visitors.

Enough Air Leakage

"The greenhouse was left untended and unwatered for five months?" you may ask incredulously. Exactly. The greenhouse is not a tight building. There is enough air leakage to provide a minimum of ventilation. Moisture condensation on the glass roof had dropped down onto the plants, keeping them minimally provided with water.

If the lettuce plants had been left in flats on benches they would certainly have dried up, but they were in beds on ground soil, at the same level as the outside garden. They therefore received some moisture from the ground up. These plants had been conditioned to expect little or no moisture and so were able to go on living under semi-desert conditions. The plants obviously got enough moisture to be able to survive.

In a previous chapter we emphasized the need of plant nourishment from the soil. In this chapter we have stressed light, heat, moisture, and air. Taken together these five elements provide the environment in which seeds germinate and in which plants grow. Aside from these aspects of plant environment there are other less tangible factors in the environment of a plant.

Talking to His Plants

A New York City artist had a greenhouse on his penthouse roof, with a gardener to take care of the plants. One day the owner overheard the gardener talking to his plants, praising some of them and chastising others for not doing better, but chatting with them all.

Said the artist to his gardener: "You old fool! Have you gone crazy? The idea of talking to a plant!" The gardener replied: "Aren't the plants alive? They breathe, drink, take nourishment, feel pleasure, and are sad. Each one is a little individual. I think it does them good to talk to them. Why

not try it yourself and see the results?" The artist became
a convert and an enthusiast for plant conversations.

Some people are observed to have a way with plants, sometimes called a "green thumb." They tend their plants phys-
ically; they also have rapport with them, undoubtedly com-
mending them and urging them on, stimulating them to do
better.

The case for plant reactions to emotional and verbal stimuli may not yet be proved to everyone's satisfaction. It is still an issue over which heated arguments are being exchanged. However, if there is a reasonable doubt, why not (as the gardener suggested) give the plants the benefit of the doubt? If special attention encourages plants, and if we wish to make a success of a greenhouse under circumstances which subject plants to special stresses and strains such as extreme temperature variations, might it not be wise to give the plants in question every possible advantage that may increase their capacity to survive? Certainly they will not be harmed by personal attention and consideration, and it is likely they may be helped.

Why Not?

It is the task of the gardener to discover by experiment and through experience what circumstances are best adapted to the needs of particular plants. While sun, air, moisture, and warmth are conditions necessary for the growth of all plants, the quality, quantity, and relationship differ from season to season and from plant to plant.

For each plant there is a combination of light, air, and warmth that is best. We know that adequate light and warmth, sufficient nourishment, moisture, and proper ventilation are essential to greenhouse well-being. Let us be open to any and every innovation which will give our plants better life and better growth.

"To me Spring is a movement, a mighty surging upward. It isn't coaxed from above, but moved from below. The growing things break upward through the crust of chill earth the way a man gets out of bed on a zero morning—gradually, reluctantly, cover by cover, a toe at a time; not because someone has waked him, but because he has accumulated the necessary refreshment of sleep and is ready to go forth and do the day's work."

Richardson Wright, *Truly Rural*, 1922

7

The greenhouse in spring

Our spring gardening time begins in late February or early in March, extending through April and May and early June. It varies with the weather and the state of the greenhouse soil. If the soil is frozen hard we must wait until it can be worked. Although the outside world may be still in the grip of snow and ice we can usually find sections protected by mulch or by the north wall which can be worked quite early.

We prepare the beds carefully, enriching the soil of the greenhouse sufficiently to give the involved seeds a bit more growing-urge than the regular greenhouse soil provides. Plants respond to encouragement in the form of extra fertilization, but as in every relation with the processes of growth, the famous Greek axiom "nothing too much" applies. The greenhouse soil should be rich enough to encourage plants, but not so rich that the plants are being forced.

Well-Ripened Compost

For this purpose our main reliance is on well-ripened compost, that is, compost which is no longer warmed by its own fermentation and which is so completely friable that when the fingers are run through it, it separates like any other dry meal.

83

Besides this compost we add a generous sprinkling of our protein meal composed of equal parts of soybean meal or cottonseed meal or linseed meal, granite dust and a finely ground phosphate rock, plus an equal part of finely ground dolomite limestone. Compost and protein meal are worked thoroughly into the soil with a potato hook or long-toothed rake until the added ingredients have disappeared into the top three or four inches of the soil.

We plant in rows about seven inches apart, marking each row with a wooden marker giving the name of seed and date. In general, we do not hope to get plants for the garden by this very early planting. What we do hope to get are small three- or four-inch seedlings which we can use—root, stem and first few leaves—for garnish on soups or for early salads.

Enough Protection

As the tiny plants appear above the ground, a hard freeze would destroy them if they were in the open. The cold greenhouse gives enough protection to enable the miniscule plants to survive the late night frosts, and warms them throughout the day. In the days that follow, with the sun getting daily higher, the sun-heated greenhouse will be anywhere up to 25° or 30° warmer than outside air. At night, while temperatures are below freezing in the open garden, the greenhouse glass shields the plants against the setback of a night frost.

With early spring weather, usually early March, we can begin planting in small seed flats for later transplantation to

BUILDING & USING OUR SUN-HEATED GREENHOUSE

garden flats or to the outside garden. We usually begin with lettuce, cabbage, celery, parsley, and spinach.

We keep a good reserve of flats which we make ourselves—both small wooden boxes for seeds and regular garden flats in which to set the tiny seedling transplants.

Garden Flats
Our regular garden flats are 15″ x 16″ x 3″. They consist of two end pieces of ¾-inch pine to which we nail side and bottom pieces of half-inch rough unplaned cedar, just as it comes from the mill. The side pieces are 3″ wide. The bottoms are made of several pieces, at least three or four, of varying widths. All the pieces are separated by a ¼-inch crack, to provide air and to prevent waterlogging.

We spread a half-inch layer of dry sphagnum moss over the bottom of all our flats and then fill with our potting soil. The potting soil is a mixture of equal quantities of ripe compost, rotted sod, pit sand, and friable garden dirt, sifted and mixed. To this mixture we add a sprinkling of our homemade nitrogen concoction, the chief constituent of which is soybean meal.

Marker
When a garden flat is being filled, we shake down the potting mixture, fill it to the top, firm it down with the hand and dampen the soil. Then we use a specially made marker which makes holes for the tiny transplants. This is an ingenious little contraption which neighbors thought up for a birthday present.

We try many varieties of lettuce, carefully marked.

The marker consists of a piece of soft wood, ¼ inch smaller than the inside dimensions of our garden flats. On one side there is a large rough handle. On the other side are set half-inch dowel pins 1 ¼″ long, driven into twenty-five equidistant holes, bored in a pattern of five rows and five dowel pins in each row. If the soil in the flat is damp and has been firmed down, one stroke with this pattern locates the holes into which the seedlings are to go.

As soon as the seedlings in the greenhouse ground or in the seed flats have put out four leaves, and if their tap roots are an inch long and have a satisfactory cluster of feeding roots, we transplant them into the garden flats.

Filled With Flats

By early April the greenhouse is filling up with flats and with beds of seeds planted directly into the greenhouse soil. After early April the chances of hard freezing are so remote that we can risk putting our flats out on the garden wall or along the edge of the garden for daily airings.

Seed planted in the greenhouse has several weeks' lead over the same seed planted in the open garden. In the greenhouse the seeds will germinate and grow, perhaps slowly, perhaps rapidly, all through the month or six weeks of night frosts that plague an open New England garden during March, April, and well into May.

Some plants, radishes, for example, will mature and be ready to eat within about twenty-five days from planting. Some others may take a bit longer. If not eaten for early spring salads, cabbage, collards, spinach, and early lettuce plants will be well-rooted seedlings and ready to be set out into flats or the open garden at the earliest practicable date.

Dry Autumn Leaves

For the first spring challenge to Jack Frost have at hand a basket containing dry autumn leaves. If frost threatens tender seedlings, either in the greenhouse or outside, a light sprinkling of the leaves over the entire scene of operations will do wonders in the way of protection. If the leaves get in the way of growth of the tender seedlings, brush them to one side in the daytime and keep them handy to be replaced on the next cold night. In doing this methodically you are only doing what nature does more or less at random on any breezy day when gusts of wind pile protecting leaves among growing plants.

If a severe late frost should wipe out seedlings which have only just broken ground in the greenhouse, proceed as soon as the ground thaws to try again. Only a small amount of seed and labor are involved in this early venture. If it is wiped out 100 percent, try, try again. The chances are that only a part of your germinating seeds will be destroyed. There may be survivors in your rows. There is at least a fair chance that your initial sally into spring gardening will produce positive results that you could not have achieved without the protection of your sun-heated greenhouse.

If the worst possible weather break destroys all your initial venture at spring gardening in the greenhouse, gather your forces for a second and if necessary a third or fourth venture.

Sooner or a little later you will get started. As the sun moves higher and the nights are less cold, your soil will gradually warm up, the air in the greenhouse will be warmer, and almost before you know it there will be a sheen of soft green all over your planted area.

On March 1, 1977 we rounded out one of the most consistently cold winters in the memory of the oldest inhabitant. Night after night during December, January, and February temperatures had ranged from the mid-twenties down to sub-zero. Days had been partly cloudy to overcast. Nights had been clear and beautiful to tempestuous. Since the first of the year the snow cover over the garden had been unbroken. There had been no January thaw and none in February.

We early spring gardeners decided that we would get a break in March and decided to begin our spring planting in the greenhouse. On March 3 we laid out two beds, each about twenty-five square feet in area. Next to the north wall the soil was still frozen. Elsewhere in the two selected areas we brushed aside the thin layer of dry leaves, working over the soil with a rake and shovel.

Deep in Snow

Our compost piles were deep in snow and frozen hard. Our compost reserve saved over from the autumn was exhausted, so we decided to plant without adding compost. We scattered a dressing of protein meal, worked it well in the soil, and began planting. The soil was moderately dry and not at all sticky. When we planted in mid-afternoon the outside temperature was 32 degrees; within the greenhouse it was 39.

We planted Scarlet Button radishes, mustard, two rows of kale, Egyptian beets, two rows of elephant leeks, a row of summer turnips, two rows of spinach, three rows of Chinese cabbage, a row each of Wakefield cabbage, broccoli, Brussels sprouts and summer Pascal celery. There was no watering at that time.

On March 9 and 10, we had our first two warmish days since October. The snow settled noticeably and spots of soil began to show in the garden. At noon on March 10 the temperature outside was 40°. The reading in the greenhouse at 2 p.m. was 77°. The back of winter was finally broken. And inside the greenhouse, the austere bed was breaking ground.

Fully
Occupied

By April and May the spring greenhouse should be fully occupied by:

First, seed flats of onions, leeks, cabbages, collards, kale, celery, celeriac, lettuce, parsley. If you are anxious to get an extra early taste of beets and carrots, a couple of rows of thinly planted beets and carrot seed planted in April and transplanted into the open garden as soon as weather permits will provide a small early crop.

The onions and beets, transplanted from the greenhouse into the open garden as soon as the garden soil is comfortably warm, will have several weeks of head start over seeds planted in the open garden. Celery and celeriac planted in a seed flat will be ready to transplant into the garden in six weeks. A seed flat of four or five kinds of lettuce planted thinly and covered with a board for the first five days (or until the seedlings break ground) will give lettuce transplants early in May.

Second, any seed flat seedlings that have developed a cluster of feeding roots and a tap root at least an inch long can go into garden flats—about twenty-five plants per garden flat. This applies to tomatoes, peppers, the cabbage family, eggplant, okra.

Third, hardy plants in flats: cabbage, lettuce, endive can be hardened off by having the flats placed in a sheltered locale for a couple of cold spells. Once hardened off, they can be moved into their rows in the outside garden.

Fourth, semi-hardy seedlings of cabbage, lettuce, endive, and the like can be moved to a sheltered position on the south side of a garden wall, hardened off on chilly nights and made ready for transplanting into the open garden.

Fifth, tomato, pepper, cucumber and melon seeds can be sown thinly in seed flats or pots six to eight weeks before they are to be set in the open garden.

The drastic transition from spring chill to comforting summer warmth has been made in the North Temperate Zone year after year for ages. Again this year, in March and April, gardeners must prepare for the transformation as the sun moves higher and the sunshine grows stronger and more insistent, first in the sheltered greenhouses, then in the outside gardens. From the sheltered valleys to the more exposed uplands, from gardens and meadows to hillsides and mountains the warmth will spread and green will again become earth's color.

Drastic Transition

"From yonder fields of aether fair disclos'd,
Child of the Sun! illustrious Summer comes,
In pride of youth, and felt thro' Nature's depths.
He comes, attended by the sultry Hours,
And ever-fanning Breezes, on his way;
While, from his ardent look, the turning Spring
Averts her blushful face, and earth, and skies,
All-smiling, to his hot dominion leaves."

James Thomson, *The Seasons,* 1730

8

The summer greenhouse

From late May to early June our spring greenhouse is being gradually replaced by our summer greenhouse. As each spring greenhouse row or bed is emptied, preparations for the summer greenhouse are started.

Perhaps you will wonder whether it is worth while to bother with a greenhouse in summertime. Why not just use the garden, you may ask. Our answer is unequivocal: We need and use the greenhouse in summer as we need and use it during all four seasons. The summer greenhouse proves its worth by providing us with abundant crops of heat-loving plants such as tomatoes, sweet peppers, eggplants, and melons.

In daytime summer heat the greenhouse may seem hardly necessary. Indeed, there are summer days when the glass concentrates so much heat that it may cause plants to wilt in the early afternoon. Some gardeners protect against such heat by brushing a water whitewash over the entire glass surface and thus reducing the severity of the summer sun rays. Our sun never gets that hot.

Cool Nights

In a New England summer there are many foggy days and cool nights when greenhouse warmth is welcomed by sensitive plants. In July and August, on the Maine coast, south and east winds bring in the fog banks. We have seen a July with only five days of full sunshine. Most of the month the sun was behind clouds, only occasionally breaking through mists day after day. Under such conditions the greenhouse is a lifesaver for plants like tomatoes and melons, peppers and eggplants which require warm nights and hot days to ripen their fruits. They also need a long growing season. Started in the spring greenhouse they are well advanced by the time summer comes along.

The summer greenhouse enables us to get early tomato plants started weeks before they could be set in the open garden. Our regular practice is to set a dozen or two early tomato plants in the greenhouse sometime in May or early June. Then, as the space opens up and the soil of the greenhouse is readied for summer use, we set out tomato plants, then pepper plants until two-thirds of the summer greenhouse is occupied by tomatoes and peppers.

Greenhouse Tomatoes

Presently on the market are several greenhouse tomatoes which bear large crops of medium-sized fruit. There is also a sugar tomato about an inch in diameter which bears its blossoms in long racemes—as many as fifteen tomatoes on a single fruit stem. We have found them ideal for greenhouse use.

We aim to take full advantage of the new varieties that seedmen introduce each year. We have been experimenting recently with several yellow tomatoes, such as Golden Queen, which do well in the greenhouse. They are more solid and less acid than their red relatives. They also keep the longest in our cellar when harvested before frost.

We have been setting the tomato plants across the entire floor of the greenhouse at distances of twenty-four to thirty inches between plants. This allows no space for a path. Instead, we walk between the plants, using first one and then another route. In this way the entire distance between the greenhouse walls can be utilized for growing plants. There is no need to waste space in paths.

We place a light stake on the north side of each tomato plant and tie the plant to it as the plant grows up the stake. As the highest point in our greenhouse is eight feet and the lower side around seven feet, we have space for tall plants to reach the roof, with a crop of fruit right to the top.

As the sun heat is intense directly under the glass roof, we prune off all tomato leaves or shoots a few inches down. We also aim to keep tomato plants free of the green side-shoots that develop and would turn into extraneous tops. By cutting out these suckers and allowing only fruiting stems to grow, the full energy of the plant goes into fruit production, not new tops. We squeeze off these extra shoots whenever we see them developing.

Several Problems

The summer greenhouse raises several problems. We want to fill the whole greenhouse with tomatoes and green peppers, eggplants and melons during June, July, and August, so our first problem is to make space. We meet that demand by moving into the open garden every movable item, such as stray leftover plants, or seed and garden flats, which find new homes on the south side of the stone wall that borders our garden on the north, or in the main garden rows.

Other problems present themselves. Under the heat of the summer sun there is rapid evaporation of moisture. We need the hot sun to germinate seeds and to produce growth, blossoming, and fruiting, but the hotter the sun the greater the evaporation, both from the plants and from any part of the garden floor exposed to the sun's rays. Watering becomes a first charge on greenhouse labor time in the summer greenhouse, particularly when transplanting.

Ventilation

Ventilation of the overheated greenhouse has become a must. If the heat is too intense and if it promises to last, the sash can be removed from the front of the greenhouse and put into storage. If left in place, it should be opened fully.

Everything grows madly in the summer. The heat, moisture, and nourishment in the soil which produce flowering and fruiting of our plants and seedlings also aid the growth of weeds. Grasses and perennial weeds that have escaped the gardener's watchful eye are up to their usual tricks. Some hide in out-of-the-way places, while others grow blatantly in the planted rows. It is up to the gardener to remove these "plants out of place." "So ply your hoes and give the weeds no peace," wrote Virgil in 37 B.C.

It is necessary to keep plants picked so that mature crops are utilized and space is gained for the new crop. At this midsummer season the entire garden, including the greenhouse, is totally engaged in producing food. Each day a generous supply of garden produce should go to the kitchen.

Shift to Autumn Gardening

The summer greenhouse also must be prepared for the shift from summer to autumn gardening. In late August the nights may be getting cold. In August or September tomato plants

Windows are wide open in summer.

that have been bearing since June or July cease blossoming and the foliage begins to dry up. At this point we remove the plant and prepare the open earth surface for its autumn garden occupants. If possible on the same day as the clearing out, the part of the greenhouse vacated by removals is filled by new arrivals, so that the space is fully occupied.

During the turnover from summer greenhouse to autumn greenhouse we remove 15 to 20 percent of greenhouse soil and take it to the composting area for use in future compost piles. In its place we put new compost, forest soil, and partly rotted autumn leaves, together with an application of our protein meal, plus a sprinkling of ground dolomite limestone. In this way we avoid soil exhaustion and add a bit more depth and fertility to our greenhouse soil.

Garden Flats   Seed flats of lettuce, curly endive, broccoli, and early cabbage will be planted. In the course of two weeks, if all goes well, three or four dozen garden flats will be planted with the seedlings growing from these flats. They are designed to be transplanted into the open garden for a few weeks, and then in October and November heeled into the greenhouse to provide an abundance of greens for the deep freeze of November, December, and January.

Late in August or early September, when the tomatoes are out, we will pick an out-of-the-way corner about two feet by four feet, and broadcast two sections of wheat seed and another of rye, raking in the seed and fertilizer with a potato hook. A few days or a week of good weather will bring the earliest shoots of the wheat and rye grass that will enrich and flavor our salads right through fall and into early winter. Young sprouts of wheat and rye, chopped fine, are a supplement and variant to our salad and soup supplies. A patch of wheat and rye will require little or no attention, although the bed may need watering like any other part of the greenhouse. A mulch of dry autumn leaves will help the young sprigs to get through a dry season. Once they have taken firm root, wheat and rye cling doggedly to life.

The summer greenhouse produces mature fruits for the kitchen. It produces young plants for the autumn garden. It also provides in August and September the seedlings that will meet the requirements of the autumn garden.

"When the silver habit of the clouds
Comes down upon the autumn sun, and with
A sober gladness the old year takes up
His bright inheritance of golden fruits,
A pomp and pageant fill the splendid scene."

Henry Wadsworth Longfellow, *Delights of Autumn*, 1841

9

The greenhouse in autumn

Through the summer the greenhouse has been pushed into the background by the abundant crops produced in the outside garden. Greens of every variety, early and midsummer root crops, tomatoes, berries, and tree fruit have kept the larder supplied with tasty edibles.

With the rush of summer gardening over and with frosty weather still several weeks in the future, the gardener cannot do better than to preserve the surpluses of tomatoes from the greenhouse and outside, and the greens that may be going to waste in the garden. Now is the time to fill the freezers, to prepare the juices for canning, to put up the quotas of soup stock and applesauce.

Night Frosts

With light night frosts possible in late August and September the summer begins to bow itself out and Jack Frost gets one foot inside the garden gate. Root crops and fruits are plentiful. The garden is still a mass of green. But summer has had its day and knows it. As each day meets twilight a few minutes earlier than its predecessor it carries an announcement that anyone can read: autumn is at hand.

109

The summer greenhouse, with a full and blooming garden outside, may have seemed extraneous. If there had been no greenhouse, the hot days and nights of July and August would have ripened the tomatoes and filled out the melons, even outside. But now the greenhouse begins to count.

In its first few days, autumn is deceptively like summer. But the autumn colors on the trees underline the warning of the night thermometer that colder days and nights are just around the corner. Soon after Labor Day autumn begins to edge its way into the picture. As the days grow shorter and the nights grow longer we begin our preparations for dealing with the

Big Freeze which will be making our fingers tingle within a brief forty or fifty days. After the heat of late July and August it seems improbable that within a few weeks we will see snowflakes drifting down, but such is the New England autumn which leads us each year from the balmy days of summer to the ice crystals and snowbanks of winter.

Pays Off

When chilly nights come we close up the greenhouse windows and begin to get nervous for our beans and tomatoes and other tender crops outside. Finally, before the first real killer frost comes, we strip our bean plants and bring into the house every green tomato. Then is when the autumn greenhouse pays off, and continues to ripen tomatoes and peppers under glass for weeks after they are gone from the outside garden.

In the September-October part of autumn we face three greenhouse duties:

1. As the tomato plants come out and greenhouse free space becomes available it should be filled with appropriate seed rows or garden transplants or seed flats.

2. We must transplant from seed flats into garden flats or from the open garden into the greenhouse such plants as may be needed for the kitchen or for the winter greenhouse, or for greenhouse replacements.

3. We must continue to plant seed flats of lettuce and beds of radishes, turnips, collards, and mustard in any vacant greenhouse area.

Until late September or early October, as greenhouse space becomes available it will be cleared of weeds and rubbish, fertilized, worked over and prepared for the late autumn plantings in the ground of broccoli, spinach, collards, kale, and red and white radishes. At this late season the seeds will germinate more slowly or not at all. In any case they will lack the vitality and vigor of the same or similar seeds planted in spring or early summer. Days are cooler and shorter, and nights are longer and colder. In the spring the seeds push; in the late autumn they lag.

Why Plant?

Under these conditions, why plant at all? Why not let the garden and greenhouse go by and wait till spring? We continue to plant as long as seeds will continue to germinate and grow. We are planting for home use, not for money or market. If it is difficult to grow seedlings and young plants late in the autumn, if they are neither as colorful nor as tasty as similar seeds planted months earlier, they still do supply green material for soups and salads.

We have planted seeds in the open garden as well as in the greenhouse right through the autumn from September to the first snowfall, either in November or December. Beets, turnips, cabbage, lettuce, spinach, and mustard have all had a chance to see what they can do.

We now know that we have greatly underestimated the capacity of many hardy greens to survive winter weather. Seedlings of cabbage, lettuce, spinach, and the like will endure and survive long spells of real winter weather, with a light mulch of dry leaves as sole protection.

In 1976 we took particular interest in such plantings all through the autumn. The weather was perfect for our purposes. During the entire period the weather was colder than average Maine October and November weather. At the same time, with the exception of a few incidental flurries, there was no snowfall to complicate our experiment as we continued to plant week after week, as long as the earth was unfrozen.

Doing Nicely   Throughout the entire September-December period the seeds in every planting, both in the greenhouse and outside, germinated and broke through the earth's surface. Individual plants in some of the earlier plantings grew as much as three inches in height. In the entire experiment there was not a single crop failure. On the contrary, the young plants in the garden were doing nicely when the deep freeze began during the second week in November and never let up till spring 1977. During cold nights the seedlings in the open ground cowered down to earth. The next morning's sun thawed them out and they stood up as vigorously as though a whole growing season were before them. Had our greenhouse been extensive enough to cover the entire outdoor experiment, we are convinced that a substantial number of all of these plants, like the greenhouse ones, would have survived the ordeal.

Our chief greenhouse job of early September is to transplant lettuce, cabbages, and endive from the seed flats in which

Ready for winter in the greenhouse.

they are growing into the garden flats which will be their home through the fall and early winter. Throughout the late autumn, seedlings which have acquired a cluster of good feeding roots can be transplanted into garden flats and later set in the greenhouse floor and carried through the winter, heading up nicely in the early spring.

From garden flats or from plantings in the late summer garden we will select some sturdy broccoli, Early Wakefield cabbage and collards and set them about eight inches apart in the greenhouse, two or three dozen plants in all. They will grow and mature in both the autumn and winter greenhouses. Young kale and lettuce plants thinned from seed rows will add to the supply of available greens. Young spinach and endive plants will be equally useful.

Every eight or ten days in the fall, as is usual through the summertime, we prepare and plant our lettuce seed flats. But we omit the summer lettuce varieties, sowing instead some Black-Seeded Simpson for a short crop, some Buttercrunch and Green Boston for a main crop, and Romaine to meet the vagaries of autumn weather. As these germinate and make good root systems we will continue to plant lettuce seed flats for several more weeks.

Semi-Hardy Plants

As autumn moves toward winter, a semi-hardy Temperate Zone plant, hardened off by repeated exposure to the progressively colder weather of late October and November, should not be seriously damaged by frost in the autumn greenhouse. There will be cold nights, of course, and even some cold days, but semi-hardy plants aided by greenhouse protection can handle such weather without difficulty.

One of the chief tasks of the gardener in autumn is to make the necessary preparations for the hard freezes that will begin in November and early December. The successful accomplishment of that task is the real test of the sun-heated greenhouse.

There is one illustrative gardening episode which could come under either our Spring, Summer or Autumn heading. It has to do with spring growth, summer planting and autumn produce. Members of two local garden clubs have held occasional

monthly meetings at our farm. A tour of the garden and greenhouse was always included. One of their meetings here was late in October. The garden and greenhouse were still full of greenery, with hardly an empty row. The ladies exclaimed, "How can you carry through so many vegetables so late in the season? Our gardens are either empty or full of nothing but weeds. Your garden looks like spring!"

We explained that seeds of plants that will survive cold weather, planted in spring, can also be planted in late summer to handle autumn's chills. In midsummer we plant again all the spring crops: radishes, spinach, collards, escarole, endive, lettuces, especially Cos, that will ripen and thrive in the cool fall weather. That is why our summer-planted garden looks like spring in the fall.

"The thing in gardening most often overlooked and neglected is the late summer planting for fall use. All those vegetables that require cool weather—lettuce, radishes, spinach, peas, etc.—will flourish in the cool of fall quite as well as in the cool spring."*

* Henry Tetlow, *We Farm for a Hobby,* 1938.

"See, Winter comes, to rule the varied year,
Sullen and sad, with all his rising train,
Vapours, and Clouds, and Storms.
Be these my theme."

James Thomson, *The Seasons,* 1730

10

The winter greenhouse

New England wintertime has usually been ruled out as ungardenable unless it is undertaken in artificially heated glass houses. Our greenhouse is unheated save by direct and indirect rays from the sun. Nevertheless we eat out of our sun-heated greenhouse right through the roughest and toughest winters. How do we do it? We have learned how to live with and prevail against winter's hazards.

The first hazard, of course, is the cold weather. Where we live in eastern Maine, along the coast, the normal winter thermometer goes below zero many times each year. Most of our plants left in the garden crumple up and rot after a hard frost. Other plants, after freezing, thaw out time after time. The first task of the would-be winter greenhouser is to find out which plants will and which will not stand hard freezing. We have been studying this matter for the last forty years and are glad to share our findings.

The second hazard is snow and ice. Snowfall may be a problem in its own right; it is certainly an effective check on gardening. Its after-effects may be even more serious. A New England

Second Hazard

121

snowstorm, driving in from the northeast, may include rain which melts part of the snow. If the storm ends by a wind shift into the north, the resulting drop in temperature turns slush and snow into a treacherous ice sheet that covers trees, highways, gardens, and footpaths. Work in the open is brought to a halt, with foot passengers and drivers alike picking their way with care, or calling it a time to hibernate.

Equipped with a glass roof a greenhouse is especially hampered by snow and ice. A snowstorm cuts off light; it also adds to the roof load. If the snow is freezing as it falls, it hardens onto the greenhouse roof and stays there until it is softened up eventually by higher temperatures. We aim to keep the greenhouse roof clear of snow. We have a wooden snow-pusher with a long, light handle. As soon as snow has had a chance to soften up on the roof we push it off and let in the light.

Ground Frozen

A third winter hazard is ground frozen so hard that it cannot be worked in the unheated greenhouse. This situation is avoided or postponed by sprinkling, before the ground hardens, a moderate layer of dry autumn leaves over any greenhouse earth that is not covered by foliage. A little experience will show how thick the layer of dry leaves should be. We know that if lettuce and other such plants have a light mulch of dry autumn leaves thrown on them it helps them to survive. Even on a sub-zero night the ground covered by such a mulch may be unfrozen.

A home-made snow-pusher keeps the roof clear.

We have checked this point on a bit of land covered by a thick growth of soft maple, white birch, and pin cherry. If the normal leaf cover on such a piece of woodland is undisturbed there will be two or three inches of dry leaves that can be kicked aside, revealing an unfrozen forest floor. Unless the ground is water-soaked, the leaves have curled up and are able to keep large air spaces between leaves which prevent the ground from freezing.

If any of the soil in the cultivated area of the greenhouse is exposed, keep it stirred up with a light stick or a small tool, even when it looks as dry as dust. Really dry ground cannot freeze; it is the water in the ground that freezes.

Another hazard is the succession of freezings and thawings that the plants may have to undergo in an unheated greenhouse. One or two such experiences may not prove fatal; too many might finish off delicate plants. The foliage of most hardy or semi-hardy plants will survive a great deal of freezing and thawing unless they have juicy stems or other exposed parts that get iced up. Deal with this difficulty by not touching frozen, brittle plants that may break off before they thaw.

We do not want to emphasize only the negative aspects of the problem. Our concern is to point out that New England plants and New Englanders themselves have lived through many winters and face many more with equanimity if properly sheltered.

New England is filled with shrubs and trees, both evergreen and deciduous, that flourish in summers and survive fierce winters. In addition, there are many grasses and other forms of vegetation that flower during hard winters. Chickweed is a good example. Grasses freeze in winter but the roots and the growing centers live on and at the first opportunity resume their growth processes. In the garden, parsnips, salsify, Jerusalem artichokes and many other plants lose their leaves and stems in winter but retain their growing centers. Tuberous roots survive severe cold and even seem to benefit by it.

Some Plants Survive Fierce Winters

In a word, we inhabitants of the North Temperate Zone are surrounded by a vast number of vegetable species that take sub-zero winter temperatures in their stride and welcome each returning spring by growing again, and flowering and fruiting. This is the process that has covered the hills and valleys of North Temperate regions for centuries with a spectacular green carpet.

If it is possible to survive bitter winter weather in the open countryside, how much easier it should be, with some care and management, to carry a greenhouse, though unheated, full of selected vegetation, from autumn through winter to spring.

We have mentioned parsnips, salsify, and Jerusalem artichokes as examples of winter survival of plants whose leaves and stems become frozen in winter. The point of our greenhouse is to assure survival of as many plants as possible *with* their green tops, stems, and leaves.

Elephant Leek

We might begin with a member of the onion family, the elephant leek. Sometimes a good example of leek will live right through the winter in an open garden. That has happened with us but we can never guarantee it. On the contrary, in our climatic belt the chances are against leek survival in the open garden.

We have found a method of protecting our leeks and keeping them green all winter. Early in November, before hard ground freeze-up, we pick up individual leek plants with a spade or shovel, keeping the roots as nearly intact as possible, and carry them to the greenhouse. There we replant the leek in a trench five or six inches deep, tramping the earth around the roots. We repeat this operation, bringing a spadeful of earth with each plant, packing them tightly together in rows and then watering them. The "heeling-in" process will preserve the life of the plant for months, during which time we bring plants as needed into the kitchen.

"Heeling-in" is a well-established practice among gardeners who want a plant to stay alive and in good condition during a waiting period, after which they can put the plant in its permanent home. We have merely extended this practice into the greenhouse, trying out a technique for transplanting mature, hardy plants of various kinds from the open garden into the greenhouse and carrying them for months through hard winter weather.

Ready to Eat

In the autumn of 1975 we had a thriving bed of elephant leeks, seeded in the greenhouse in April, transplanted to the garden in May. In early November the leeks were as large as your wrist, frozen up on cold nights and thawing out a bright green on sunny days. They were ready to eat but there were too many to eat all at once. We wanted to keep them edible all winter if possible. So on a warm afternoon we moved a hundred plants into the greenhouse.

In taking them up we found two or three plants had so intertwined their roots that it was difficult to pull them apart. Leeks have large systems of long and strong roots. Instead of trying to separate them by breaking them apart, we took a pair of plants at a time, moved the whole section into the greenhouse, dug an enlarged hole and pressed the root mass into place, covering the roots and firming the earth. During the transplanting operation no leek leaves wilted. And during the next three to four months, while we were using up the leeks, not a single leek plant died in the greenhouse.

The same heeling-in technique was applied to some mature strawberry chard plants which had distinguished themselves by the length and thickness of their leaf stems. All chard plants took the transplanting well, but most of them froze down in a later period of sub-zero weather. Chard leaf stems are filled with plenty of water, so perhaps we were lucky to save one, which to our surprise and delight lasted through the incredible winter and began growing vigorously in late March. It will be like eating a pet hen to consume this one.*

Lettuce

We come now to lettuce, which is very important to us because we use it so frequently in salad making, and go out of our way to have this tender fresh green for at least one meal every day. But can it be grown through a New England winter? In a 1563 book we found the following:

"Lettys maye be sowen all the yeare through, and mingled together with other herbes, and that, which shall be sowen in harvest may very well be set againe in the moneth of December and in beddes with other herbes: for it wel abydeth the cold winter tyme, and ys also muche strenthened thereby, and it shall be good with other herbes unto the sede tyme."†

---

* We never did eat it. We let it grow until it touched the roof, eight feet high, and went to seed. We hope to cooperate with successive generations of this magnificent plant.
† Thomas Hyll, *A Most Briefe and Pleasant Treatyse.*

Lettuce is a rather fussy cold weather plant. During a zero night the entire lettuce plant is frozen stiff. When the sun thaws out the plants, those with thin leaf stems continue green and alive and go on living normally. After several freezings, lettuce with thick leaf stems begins to rot. The leaf stems in Oak Leaf lettuce, for example, are relatively thin. The stems of Simpson lettuce also are thin; the leaf stems of Romaine are juicy. The Butterhead lettuces generally have moderately thick leaf stems.

As our experiments have proceeded we have found that Simpson, Oak Leaf, Green Boston, Buttercrunch, and other lettuces with particularly dry leaf spines have survived during our Maine winters. With one exception (the winter of 1975–76) we have succeeded in carrying some at least of our lettuce plants through every winter. Almost always they went into winter as half-grown plants or even plants still in garden flats.

Our lettuce plants still in shallow garden flats were wiped out the winter of 1976–77 while those in beds survived. Weathermen counted ten distinct storm cycles from the middle of November 1976 to the end of February 1977. These storms followed one another closely, without a single thaw break. In the severest weather the curly endive and escarole were retarded but did not die. Their growth was checked but they were not killed by weeks and months of sub-zero frost.

All Plants Survived

We would like to refer especially to a bed of broad-leafed Batavian escarole which we raised in a seed flat and then transferred to a garden flat. They were three inches high when moved into a greenhouse bed and covered with autumn leaves. All of these plants survived the same winter that killed the lettuce which was in flats.

As we pass this unusually persistent and prolonged winter season in review, we are pleased we went through it before we wrote this book. Despite its extreme severity we can report that we were able to carry a variety of vegetable greens through one sub-zero period after another with no thaw in between. Each sub-zero cycle proved to us that our basic assumption concerning the capacity of succulent green vegetation to outlast deep freeze is established beyond question.

William Cobbett in his 1810 book, *A Year's Residence in the U.S.A.*, states: "We have had, all winter, and have now (March 31) white cabbages, green savoys, parsnips, carrots, beets, young onions, radishes, white turnips, Swedish turnips and potatoes; and all these in abundance (except radishes, which were a few to try), and always at hand at a minute's warning.... I gave two bushels and a half of Swedish turnips for one of apples; and mind, this is on the last day of March. I have here stated facts, whereby to judge of the winter."

At the other end of the equation is the recognition of the unquestioned fact that all growing things have their limits. Celery is more fragile than lettuce. Its leaf stems are thick and juicy. In the winter of 1976–77 we had a bed of celery plants which we had raised from seed, put into garden flats, and heeled into the greenhouse in the autumn of 1976. The celery plants took the transplanting well and went into the winter lightly

mulched. We then entered into the toughest winter in memory. In the course of that winter this batch of celery was completely wiped out, but it survived for more than a month with outside temperatures down to seven degrees below zero and up to that time showed little frost damage.

All Will Not Survive

It is obvious that all vegetables will not survive a winter in our sun-heated greenhouse. We selected hardy plants for our experiment and treated them as well as we could. We learned a great deal during these experiments. We found out that a homesteading family using a sun-heated greenhouse as its medium can supply itself on a twelve-month basis with salad and other greens taken directly from the garden and greenhouse. If our contention is upheld by subsequent tests, New Englanders and other cold climate homesteaders have a means of greatly improving their winter diets without dependence on artificial heating or on products imported from Florida, Texas, California, or Cuba.

Parsley

Meanwhile we are continuing our experiments with a greater variety of plants because we would like to have at least a dozen greens that will survive the Maine winter in a sun-heated greenhouse. Our guess is that much depends upon the water content of succulent leaf stems, also on the moisture content of the soil in which the plants are growing.

We know that a parsley leaf with a juicy stem will freeze, the cells will burst, and with the first warm weather the stem will begin to rot. But please note the difference between the stem and the leaf webbing. The leaf web may go on living for days and weeks despite the loss of the leaf stem support. This fact leads us to conclude that certain varieties of parsley, lettuce, and other plants, carefully selected for the relative dryness of the leaf stems, will survive, particularly if watering is reduced to a minimum.

Critics may protest that our experiments and devices for lengthening the growing season through a long winter in an unheated greenhouse involve too many operations and are too costly in labor time. It is easier to buy food in the supermarket. That may be true, but remember, we are amateur homesteaders with some free time on our hands during the sub-zero season. We are not growers for the commercial market and we have no creditors and banks yapping at our heels. And we do have a fanatical desire to supply ourselves with our own garden fresh food, even if the process requires time and some extra patience and persistence.

"And now, brother farmers, wishing you all the success which in this business, of all others, is the certain reward of industry, intelligence and enterprise, I proceed with my daily labors on my farm, trusting that with you I shall reap some advantages from the accumulated experiences of others, here compiled and condensed with my own humble observations."

Edward James Hooper, *The Practical Farmer*, 1839

11

A project for home gardeners and homesteaders

A sun-heated greenhouse is not a luxury. It is a "must" for all North Temperate homesteaders who are making a drive for self-sufficiency and who are convinced of the importance of a year-round diet of fresh greens.

In climates where frost or prolonged cold does not threaten crops, a greenhouse is expendable. But in large areas of New England, and in parts of the rest of the north country, much of the year is subject to frost. Under these conditions, any measure that will increase the number of days free from frost danger for special crops is worthy of serious consideration.

Self-Sufficient

The homesteader wishes to be self-sufficient as largely as possible in food as well as other essentials. If he is satisfied to live on potatoes and turnips from the cellar as a basic diet, a greenhouse may not be too important. If, however, the homesteader is committed to a large intake of green vegetables all year round, the greenhouse becomes indispensable. An extension of the growing season, such as a sun-heated greenhouse makes

137

possible, is a real achievement and an important addition to the life of the whole family.

One of the great advantages of homesteading is the chance for each member of the family to take part in homestead work and thus learn by doing. Everyone in the family can help build and maintain a working greenhouse. With home materials at hand (sand, gravel, rocks and timbers from the place), money need only be spent for glass, cement, and nails. None of the work need be skilled. Simple lines and sturdiness of construction are all that is needed for the greenhouse. It can be an amateur one-man job or a family undertaking.

Other advantages open up for the home gardener. "The numerous benefits resulting to every family from the production of a well-cultivated garden are too evident to need any remarks by way of illustration. The health they afford to the family, not only in the luxuries which they furnish for the table, but in the exercise, amusement and enjoyment they impart in the cultivation, exceed all description; to say nothing of the convenient profit it affords to those who are situated within reach of a market, for any surplus they may have to spare."* The greenhouse could become a possible source of monetary livelihood in a season when indoor work is usually the only occupation.

This last possibility may have meaning for families who are looking for a chance to make a living more or less on their own in the midst of a social system that is rapidly replacing

* Randolph's *Culinary Gardener*, 1826.

small farms by larger and ever larger enterprises. Granted that the large factory-like farm has its place in a society built around big and ever bigger manufacturing, mining, public utility, financial and merchandising corporate establishments, is this not an excellent reason for giving the individual gardener and farmer at least standing room in this assemblage of corporate business giants?

Early Settlers

The early settlers in this country crossed the ocean in search of adventure, of precious metals, of opportunities to escape the crowding and jostling of Europe and Asia, to get access to land on which they, their families, and dependents, could live more satisfying lives than they would have lived at home. Many of these people were homesteaders. They came to the New World looking for a better life. Today the children and grandchildren of these early homesteaders are turning from the comforts, conveniences, and questionable security with which city congestion has surrounded them, and in their turn are seeking a new place in the sun. They have turned their backs on high-rise apartments, on city crowding and congestion, on city suburbia.

Some of these people are dropouts from school or college; others are graduates, holding diplomas from higher schools or universities. Some of them have dead-end jobs and wish to change them for a more interesting way of life. Many of them are members of the eight million army of USA registered unemployed. Some of these people are young; others are in

middle life; still others are old and retired. Whatever their status, they are members of society for which the present USA economy has no satisfactory place.

When we took up homesteading in 1931, we were members of this million-strong army of the unplaced or misplaced. We acquired a ringside seat from which we could see this army on the march because so many of its members walked through our front yard. As we converted our New England place from a derelict, bankrupt farm into a thriving self-sufficient homestead, people heard about the transformation and came to have a look. At first there were few visitors, but as the years passed they grew in numbers. Among the hundreds of girls and boys, men and women who visited our Vermont homestead there were many idly curious and but few who were really looking for an answer to the problem of finding a satisfactory place in the land of their birth.

Twenty years later, when we left Vermont and moved to Maine, the army of misplaced, unplaced, and unemployed had grown in numbers and changed somewhat in its make-up. Today, among the thousands who visit our Maine homestead each year, the majority are seriously looking for an answer to the urgent question: What can we do with our lives that will be worthwhile during the years ahead?

They are no longer merely idly questioning, as they were forty years ago. They are dead serious and insistent. They are prepared to buy land; they want to find a place to settle down

Our Ringside Seat

and live out their dreams. They are out to learn the skills that are needed for survival on the new frontier in which they want to take part. They are not satisfied to be drop-outs. They are tired of drifting. They want to put down roots. Many of them are married; some have children. Some have good jobs but are tired of them. They want more out of life than a fat pay check every Friday, a comfortable home, and two cars in the garage.

During our years in Vermont the problem of finding a place to live and a way to live the good life confronted thousands. Today the same problem faces millions. As the economy matures and specializes, as the population increases year by year, the numbers of the displaced and misplaced grow faster than the population.

During the four decades that have elapsed since we staked out our claim for a good life in the green mountains of Vermont, we early homesteaders have had a whole generation of homesteading experience, learning many useful lessons by following the pattern of frontier living in colonial days. For us, one of the most important of these lessons is the possibility of making a satisfactory living with a minimum of working capital, plus a great deal of careful planning, and a considerable amount of hard physical labor.

Changes in Technology

Meanwhile we have lived through a series of changes in technology that have mechanized agriculture. The same technical advances which provided heavy industry with machinery and

Scott chats with his many young visitors.

large farms with specialized equipment have helped to make the small self-sufficient farm or homestead more practicable. Hand cultivators and lawn mowers have been made for the home gardener; light, easy-to-handle chain saws and small pickup trucks are available for the small-time farmer.

These labor-saving gadgets are purchased from the vast merchandising apparatus which advertises stridently: "We have what you want. We can supply all of your needs." There is this immense supermarket merchandising apparatus all set up and ready to supply consumer goods and services if and when consumers are willing and able to pay the overhead costs of setting up and running the mass market.

What is the alternative? Captain John Smith of the Virginia colony had the answer: If you would have a thing done well, do it yourself. If you do not want to pay the market overhead, bypass the market and provide for your needs with your own labor. This can be done when the small producers and their families are ready to do their own work, on their own time, with their own skills and under their own direction.

A Better Life

Through the ages human beings have been searching for a good life—a better life. The current movement to homestead, to live simply, quietly, in good health, in clean air and in the country is part and parcel of that long-term trend.

It is not only a movement for individual betterment; it implies social change and improvement as well. Emerson said, "He who digs a well, constructs a stone foundation, plants a grove of trees by the roadside, plants an orchard, builds a durable house, reclaims a swamp, or so much as puts a stone seat by the wayside, makes the land so far lovely and desirable, makes a fortune which he cannot carry away with him, but which is useful to his country long afterwards."*

As the determination to live a better life spreads through the North Temperate Zone, it is being transformed from a wish or dream stage into concrete social patterns. Providing fresh green

* *Society and Solitude,* 1904.

food in a sun-heated greenhouse is but one example of this advance. A large degree of self-sufficiency lies within the easy reach of any homesteaders who have established themselves and who are ready to put time, energy, and ingenuity into stabilizing their homestead way of life.

A sun-heated greenhouse is a project a New England family can work at and benefit by. The undertaking can enlarge the possibilities of income. It can extend and enlarge the variety and quality of food consumed. It can enhance the homestead itself by an attractive addition to the home buildings. It can open up a better life for its builders and for the country at large.

"Therefore all seasons shall be sweet to thee,
Whether the summer clothe the general earth
With greenness, or the redbreast sit and sing
Betwixt the tufts of snow on the bare branch."

Samuel Taylor Coleridge, *Frost at Midnight,* 1798

Other Garden Way books you will enjoy

If your goal is greater self-sufficiency, Garden Way books can help provide the information you need—on gardening, building, heating with wood or solar heating systems, raising animals, or food preparation. Here is a sample list of our books.

Low-Cost Pole Building Construction, by Douglas Merrilees and Evelyn Loveday, 102 pages, 8½ x 10½, deluxe paperback, $4.95. For sturdy yet inexpensive buildings and sheds, try this proven method.

Keeping the Harvest: Home Storage of Vegetables and Fruits, by Nancy Thurber and Gretchen Mead, 208 pages, 8½ x 11, with many illustrations, quality paperback, $5.95; hardback, $8.95. Buy this and you won't need the other food processing books. Absolutely complete.

Down-to-Earth Vegetable Gardening Know-How, featuring Dick Raymond, 160 pages, 8½ x 11, quality paperback, $5.95. Packed with practical hints, how-to lore, common-sense techniques.

Designing & Building a Solar House, by Donald Watson, 288 pages, heavily illustrated oversize paperback, $8.95. Practical how-to book just when you need it if you are considering alternate heating systems.

The Complete Book of Heating with Wood, by Larry Gay, 128 pages, quality paperback, $3.95. All the hard-to-find information in one volume.

New Low-Cost Sources of Energy for the Home, by Peter Clegg, 250 pages, 8½ x 11, heavily illustrated, quality paperback, $6.95, hardback, $8.95. New edition of this book, telling you all about alternate energy.

These books are available at your bookstore, or may be ordered directly from Garden Way Publishing, Dept. GH, Charlotte, VT 05445. If order is less than $10, please add 60¢ postage and handling.